THE *Emotional* AFFAIR

How to
Recognize
Emotional
Infidelity
and What
to Do
About It

RONALD T. POTTER-EFRON, MSW, PH.D.
PATRICIA S. POTTER-EFRON, MS

New Harbinger Publications, Inc.

Publisher's Note

Distributed in Canada by Raincoast Books

Copyright © 2008 by Ron Potter-Efron & Patricia S. Potter-Efron

New Harbinger Publications, Inc.
5674 Shattuck Avenue
Oakland, CA 94609
www.newharbinger.com

Acquired by Melissa Kirk; Cover design by Amy Shoup;
Edited by Nelda Street

Library of Congress Cataloging-in-Publication Data

Potter-Efron, Ronald T.
  The emotional affair : how to recognize emotional infidelity and what to do about it /
Ronald T. Potter-Efron and Patricia S. Potter-Efron.
     p. cm.
  Includes bibliographical references.
  ISBN-13: 978-1-57224-570-9 (pbk. : alk. paper)
  ISBN-10: 1-57224-570-0 (pbk. : alk. paper)
  1. Adultery. 2. Marriage. 3. Married people--Psych
ogy. I. Potter-Efron, Patricia S. II. Title.
  HQ806.P68 2008
  306.73'6--dc22

                         2008039780

FSC
Mixed Sources
Product group from well-managed
forests and other controlled sources

Cert no. SW-COC-002283
www.fsc.org
© 1996 Forest Stewardship Council

10 09 08

10 9 8 7 6 5 4 3 2 1   First printing

Dedication

To the newest members of our family:
Patti and Tatiany Valeriano Potter-Efron

Contents

Acknowledgments

We want to thank Jess Beebe, senior editor, and Melissa Kirk, acquisitions editor, for their assistance in developing the manuscript, and Nelda Street, our copy editor, for her thoughtful and careful work. We would also like to thank Carla Peterson, our friend and colleague, with whom we engaged in many conversations on the topic of emotional affairs that helped clarify our thinking. And, as in the past, we appreciate Matt McKay and everyone at New Harbinger, especially on this occasion in which they have entrusted us to write a book on a relatively unfamiliar topic.

Introduction

We humans are a species of bonders. From birth onward, each of us makes a concerted effort to find people with whom we can connect. Once we locate those individuals, we work hard to keep close to them, often for the rest of our lives. We form deep, powerful attachments with parents, partners, children, friends, teachers, spiritual leaders, and so on. These bonds make our lives meaningful. There's one catch though: a personal responsibility accompanies every significant attachment we make. The name for that obligation is "commitment." A commitment is a promise to those we have bonded with that we will honor our mutual relationship. We won't just walk away from a serious relationship as if it means nothing.

This book revolves around the concept of honoring our commitments. Actually, we're only focusing on one area of commitment, namely, the relationship between two adult partners that used to go by the name of marriage. Nowadays it's wiser to speak of "committed relationships" though, so that's the term we'll use herein. We're referring to long-term, usually sexual, usually heterosexual, multifaceted attachments. Partners in committed relationships also commonly want to be each other's best friend, at least in typically romanticized American courtship scenarios.

Unfortunately, sometimes one partner strays from the path of mutual commitment. The result may be a sexual affair. Who hasn't seen many a good marriage founder on the shores of that rocky shoal? Hundreds, if not thousands, of books have been written about the causes of sexual affairs, the damage they do, and attempts to repair relationships damaged by these occurrences.

Affairs are the subject of this volume but not sexual affairs. Our interest is in something far subtler than sex. Our concern is with emotional affairs. An emotional affair is defined as *an intense, primarily emotional, nonsexual relationship that diminishes at least one person's emotional connection with his or her committed partner.* Intentionally or unintentionally, participants in these affairs act like sneak thieves. The difference is that, instead of money or jewelry, these thieves purloin feelings of trust, openness, and emotional connection. Worse yet, they proceed to hand over these family treasures to someone new. They share their important thoughts and feelings with special third parties instead of with their committed partners. And then they return home and act as if nothing is wrong! They pretend, sometimes to themselves as well as to their partners, that nothing is missing in their relationships. Furthermore, they hope their partners won't notice that anything is missing. From the partner's perspective, that would be like coming home after a thief has made off with your computer, television, bed, and kitchen table and saying that everything looks fine.

Each chapter in this book is designed to answer a major question about emotional affairs. Of course, the first question is, exactly what is an emotional affair? We've already defined that term but will go into more detail about these affairs, as well as contrast them with sexual affairs, total affairs, and friendships, in chapter 1. We'll also include a questionnaire to help you decide if your partner might be having an emotional affair.

It's very stressful to realize that your life partner has become emotionally overinvolved with another. Stress is hard on both mind and body. In chapter 2 we'll examine how your partner's emotional affair may be negatively affecting you. For example, your ability to think straight might be compromised because of worry and obsession. Your emotions also might be affected, causing you to struggle with anxiety or depression. Another possibility is that you've started getting sick more often as your immune system has become overtaxed by this stressful situation. A fourth area of concern is your behavioral choices. It's easy to say and do things you later regret under these circumstances. Finally, even your spirit can be deeply affected by an emotional affair. If so, you'll find yourself becoming more pessimistic and feeling pretty hopeless about things.

Chapter 3 addresses this question: why would my partner have an emotional affair? "Why" is a difficult but important question for which there may be no single answer. We approach this issue from a commonsense perspective, namely, that apparently your partner wants something that he or she feels is absent or lacking in your relationship. We'll describe several of these desires, a few examples of which are the need for more emotional connection, understanding, praise, and emotional intensity. The idea here is to identify what's missing in your relationship, at least in your partner's eyes. Later in the book we'll describe how to use that information to benefit your partnership.

Chapter 4 addresses a particularly painful question: whose fault is it that this emotional affair is occurring? We'll look at (but reject) the most obvious responses: it's all your partner's fault, it's all your fault, and it's all the third party's fault. Instead, we'll ask you to take what's called a "systems approach." In that view, whatever happens in a system, such as your committed relationship, is about "us" as well as "me" and "you." We'll examine seven negative emotional patterns that may have developed in your relationship, any of which could've increased the emotional distance between you. Three such patterns are mutual anger and hostility, lack of emotional commitment, and focusing on the family to the point of neglecting the couple bond. Again, this information will help you improve your relationship in the long run, after the emotional affair has ended.

The first half of this book primarily centers on what's happening to you, whereas the second half deals mostly with what you can do about it. The key question in chapter 5 is how to go about challenging your partner. Essentially you need to insist decisively that he or she terminate the emotional affair. We'll describe three stages you'll go through. The first is preparation, during which you'll need to gather accurate and detailed information, develop your support system, and be able to distinguish between what you're willing to negotiate and bottom-line issues that are not subject to compromise. The second step is the action stage. Here you'll need to be assertive. We'll discuss the four *c*'s of a good intervention: being clear, concrete, concise, and controlled. Finally, your third step will be evaluative as you reflect upon your intervention, and use your support people and your self-caring to regain your strength.

We've designed this book primarily for the partner of someone having an emotional affair. However, two chapters (6 and 8) speak directly to the partner who is engaged in the emotional affair. Chapter 6 directly asks the reader, "Are you having an emotional affair?" We include a twenty-item emotional affair questionnaire there, as well as a brief description of what an emotional affair is and why it damages one's primary relationship. If your partner is willing to read just one chapter from this book, let it be chapter 6.

In chapter 7 we presume that you've gotten your message across and your partner has ended his or her emotional affair. But just stopping that affair isn't enough to get your relationship back on track. The question we try to answer here is, what do you need to do as a couple to recover from the emotional affair? We'll use an analogy, asking you to imagine that your relationship is like a house that has been damaged by a long, bad storm. We'll help you examine and improve all the rooms in that home. By the way, the names for the rooms in your house are trust, commitment, friendship, love, respect, acceptance, forgiveness, and growth. We also include a straightforward dos and don'ts list for healing after an emotional affair to guide you on this critically important home improvement project.

Lastly, the major question in chapter 8 is this: what is it about the Internet that makes it so easy for people to develop emotional affairs? We believe that the combination of intensity, immediacy, and anonymity on the Internet increases the likelihood for irresponsible behavior. This chapter has important information both for readers involved in an online emotional affair and their committed partners.

We'll close this introduction by discussing our choice of terms to describe the three people involved in an emotional affair. We considered several names for each person, trying to avoid the nastiest accusatory titles while not ducking the painful reality of this situation. The term we've decided to use most often for the person having the emotional affair is "strayer." A strayer is someone who drifts off a chosen path, often without even realizing it. However, once the strayer realizes that he or she has strayed away, it's that person's responsibility to return to the main path as quickly as possible. So, although using this term minimizes blame and shame, it doesn't alleviate someone's moral responsibilities. The name we're using for the partner who is not having the emotional affair is either just "partner" or "committed partner." The latter emphasizes the idea that this partner is, in effect, the advocate for the relationship bond. It's this individual who wants the emotional affair to end and to improve the quality of the relationship. As for the third person, the individual with whom the strayer is involved in the emotional affair, we'll just call that person the "third party." Lastly, we often use the term "committed relationship" to emphasize the sanctity of the original partnership bond.

1

Is Your Partner Having an Emotional Affair?

■ *Bill: A Thirty-Five-Year-Old Businessman*

Bill is confused. Something's wrong in his marriage with May. It all seems to have started several months ago, when May began talking a lot with her coworker Brad. Now May and Brad call each other several times a day. They usually have lunch together too, although they don't work in the same department. Even the kids have noticed. Just the other day at dinner, they asked where Mom was and why she came home so late every day.

Bill has accused his wife of having an affair with Brad. That really ticked her off though. She absolutely denies that anything sexual is going on between them. She claims she doesn't find Brad the least bit attractive that way. But she also says the reason she spends so much time with Brad is that he's never critical of her the way Bill is. She can tell Brad how she feels, what she thinks, and all the important things in her life, like her goals, fears, and dreams. She finds herself wanting to be home less and less. Her energy is directed more toward Brad than Bill.

May doesn't see why spending time with Brad should threaten her marriage. Bill doesn't see how it cannot be a threat.

Bill's wife is having an emotional affair.

◼ *Alice:* A Forty-Five-Year-Old Homemaker

Alice has fantasies of taking an ax to her husband George's computer. "You spend too much time up in your office on that machine. You're neglecting me and the kids."

Alice would be twice as upset if she realized what George has been doing upstairs. Every night, he connects with his friend Betty, a single lady with time on her hands. They go back and forth, talking about anything and everything. Mostly, George talks, and Betty responds to his long list of complaints about Alice—her disinterest in sex, her poor sense of direction, her spending habits, and on and on. He tells Betty he'd love to leave Alice but stays for the sake of the children. Afterward, George often feels guilty about having spent hours bad-mouthing his wife. But at least now, he thinks, he can get some of his emotional needs met. He feels special when he talks with Betty.

Alice's husband is having an emotional affair.

◼ *Marie:* A Twenty-Five-Year-Old Computer Programmer

Marie can sense that something's wrong. She doesn't like the feelings she gets when she sees how her husband Darren acts with his coworker Denise. They started off just talking. Denise has a child with ADHD, as do Darren and Marie, so they had a lot of common ground to begin a friendship. The more they talked, the more time they spent with each other. They knew they weren't supposed to get too close though, because their business has a rule against fraternizing. But Marie knows they sneak around that, because Darren told her once that he and Denise left work separately to meet at a restaurant for lunch. Now Darren's become secretive. He won't tell Marie what he and Denise discuss anymore. And she's seen the two of them sharing long, long hugs. Marie has always been certain she could trust Darren because he's such a devoted family man. But now she's not so sure.

Darren is having an emotional affair that could turn into a sexual affair.

■ *James: A Twenty-Year-Old College Student*

James is furious with his girlfriend Stacia. What right does she have to sit in the cafeteria smiling and chatting with Marty? Stacia is James's girlfriend. He's been thinking seriously of proposing, and there she is acting like a cheap tramp. Sure, she tells him he's got a jealousy problem, but so what? She's his girlfriend and she shouldn't be talking with any other man.

James has a problem, all right, but it's not Stacia. She is simply being friendly. She is not having an emotional affair.

WHAT IS AN EMOTIONAL AFFAIR?

Emotional affairs are amazingly complex relationships that come in many varieties, which means that no single definition can hope to completely describe them all. Nevertheless, it's possible to define emotional affairs based upon their most general characteristics. Here is our definition: *an emotional affair is an intense, primarily emotional, nonsexual relationship that diminishes at least one person's emotional connection with his or her committed partner.* Now let's pull this definition apart to look at its major components.

The Intensity of the Emotional Affair

One way emotional affairs differ from mere friendships is that the people involved in them become "positively charged." By that, we mean that people like May and Brad are strongly attracted toward each other. They look forward with great anticipation to their meetings. And when they do get together, whether face to face, by phone, or even by e-mail, they become engrossed with each other. Time flies so fast that sometimes they're late for their other duties or appointments. Perhaps because they trust each other completely, May and Brad can be totally nondefensive when they talk with each other. With no need to defend themselves, guard what they say, or look good, these two people feel unbound and newly energized. They get more than a little high just by being around each other.

The Primarily Emotional Nature of the Emotional Affair

Darren and Denise began their relationship talking about their children's problems with ADHD. They weren't just consulting about medications, doctors, and their kids' futures though. They were sharing their fears, frustrations, despair, and hopes. Denise could tell Darren how terrible she felt when her son Adam was first diagnosed with ADHD. Darren, in turn, described how he had to walk away when he first found out about his child's disorder to keep from breaking down in tears. Now though, he felt safe enough with Denise that he could, and did, cry.

One thing led to another. After a while Denise felt she could trust Darren with all her emotions. She could laugh with him about her stupid dog jumping off a cliff and somehow landing in the one patch of sand that saved him. She could get good and mad about her coworkers' ineptitude without worrying that Darren might defend them. Denise believed she could express any and all of her feelings to Darren without his ever pooh-poohing them as her husband tended to do.

It's this primacy of emotional connection that truly distinguishes emotional affairs from friendships or sexual affairs. Participants in emotional affairs have found someone with whom they can fully and completely express their emotions. That's what attracts them in the first place and keeps them there for the duration. Emotional affairs are mainly outlets for emotional release.

The Nonsexual Nature of the Emotional Affair

Brad and May are very clear about the nonsexual aspect of emotional affairs. They don't want their emotional relationship to turn into a sexual one. They may not be even remotely physically attracted to each other. However, that isn't always the case. Sometimes one or both participants are indeed erotically interested in their emotional partner. But they tend to resist such urges because basically that's not what they want from these relationships. Equally important, Brad senses that what makes his relationship with May unique and important—namely, its powerful emotionality—might get sacrificed upon the altar of sexuality if they turned in that direction.

How the Emotional Affair Diminishes Emotional Connection

Why does guilt keep nudging at George? The answer is that he has begun to realize that the energy he's been putting into his special friendship is at least partly stolen from his primary relationship. That's also why May's family is so upset with her. They're angry, because all too often, she acts more like a visitor in her home than a real family member. Like other affairs, emotional affairs can become great threats to the strayer's primary relationship when the bulk of his or her time and energy is diverted away from the partner and family.

In some ways, emotional energy is akin to the water used to irrigate farm crops. If a farmer chooses to mostly water one field, then there won't be enough for another. And, if that farmer becomes so excited about watering a new field that he or she forgets all about irrigating the older field, the crops in that field will wither and die.

George feels guilty because he realizes he's not truly working with Alice on their marriage. Instead, he complains about it to

Betty. Yes, in doing so, he feels better for a while. But ultimately he's hurting himself.

About now, you're probably asking why people get involved in these affairs. We'll discuss that question in detail later, in chapter 3. For now, let's just say that a person may choose an emotional affair as an alternative to working on his or her primary relationship, because (1) it feels better and is easier, (2) he or she currently feels somewhat hopeless about fixing problems in the primary relationship, or (3) he or she is looking to meet wants and needs perceived to be lacking in the primary relationship.

An Emotional Affair Is an Affair

We realize that calling something an "affair" is a judgment, implying that an emotional affair is a problem, a mistake, something to be stopped. We believe that emotional affairs are usually unwise relationships that do more damage than good. However, that's not to say that we don't recognize how alluring, important, and compelling they can be. It's exactly because of their power that we advise people to avoid getting into them and to seriously think about getting out of one if they're already there.

HOW EMOTIONAL AFFAIRS DIFFER FROM FRIENDSHIPS

Emotional affairs might begin as friendships, but they don't stay that way. The friendship becomes transformed, sometimes slowly, sometimes almost immediately, into a fundamentally different relationship. There are distinct differences between friendships and emotional affairs. Since we've already described emotional affairs, let's turn our attention now to defining friendship: *friendship is a mutually important but limited and nonsexual relationship based upon warm appreciation, trust, and shared interests and emotions.*

Friendship is a special bond, a wonderful kind of attachment. Of course, the idea of friendship means different things to different people. There are dozens of synonyms for the term, including camaraderie, intimacy, companionship, harmony, solidarity, fellowship, and familiarity. But one phrase best summarizes the core of a friendship: warm affection. Friends feel good spending time with each other. They like each other. They good-naturedly tolerate each other's quirks. They joke together.

Friends are people you can trust too. You can talk to them about important things, although maybe not about everything. Hopefully, good friends won't betray your trust by gossiping about you or taking advantage of your good will. If they do though, they risk losing your friendship. A friendship without trust is like a deck of cards with no aces.

Friendship usually involves sharing interests and emotions. Some friendships are weighted toward shared interests, such as a couple of guys who hunt together but rarely talk about what's going on in their lives. Other friendships center around shared feelings—for example, two individuals who met at a grief support group while mourning the loss of their spouses and then continue to see each other regularly as a way of getting on with their lives. But even friends who hardly ever discuss feelings could do so; just imagine those same two hunters sitting on tree stumps while one pours out his anguish over his wife's filing of divorce papers. Meanwhile, the two grievers might start going on trips together as they heal, instead of only talking about their difficult emotions.

Another key aspect of friendship is a prohibition against sexual connection. Sexual involvement is certainly forbidden in friendships in which one or both parties are committed to others. That's undoubtedly one reason many people limit their friendships to people they're not physically attracted to. But the taboo against sexual involvement actually is stronger than that. Many single people develop good, nonsexual friendships with other singles even when they're somewhat erotically interested in them. If you ask them why they don't move in that direction, they usually say, "I guess we could be partners. I do find him (or her) attractive. But I just value our friendship too much and am afraid getting involved that way would ruin it. I'd rather just stay friends. There's so much less tension that way."

Friendships are also bound by time and energy constraints. True, friends make wonderful additions to someone's life. They definitely make life better and richer. Still, friendships have a limited place in our lives. A friend is someone you see occasionally, perhaps as often as daily for an hour or two, or less frequently, like once a week for lunch, but not all the time. You don't go home to your friend the way you go home to your partner or spouse. You might call a friend to ask for help watching the kids or pulling out a tree stump and he or she would be happy to assist you, but not every day in every way.

We want to emphasize this point: *even the best friendship is a limited relationship.* True, friendships add spice and flavor to the soup of life, but that's all. They aren't the stock for the soup. They aren't the main ingredient. Friendships are naturally limited mutual engagements. And that means something tremendously important for the purposes of this book: friendships, even good friendships, are not usually perceived as threats to a person's marriage.

Indeed, we believe that the limitations of friendship have been unconsciously designed over hundreds of generations specifically to allow people to have both friends and spouses without animosity or conflict. For that matter, spouses who get bothered over their partners' innocent friendships are usually labeled as irrationally jealous men or women with serious insecurity issues. These people live in constant fear because they misunderstand the true nature of friendship.

So the key aspects of friendship are warm affection, trust, shared interests and emotions, a nonsexual connection, limited time and energy involvement, and the absence of any threat to the primary-relationship commitment. Now we can compare friendships with emotional affairs. They're similar in that both are primarily nonsexual relationships. They also both usually include emotional connection. But while friendships are limited in scope and energy involvement, emotional affairs are intense and demanding of energy. Most critically, friendships are carefully structured to complement the participants' primary connections, while emotional affairs drain energy, trust, and involvement away from them. Friendships don't represent a threat to a marriage. Emotional affairs are a serious threat to a person's commitment to his or her partner.

EMOTIONAL AFFAIRS VS. SEXUAL AFFAIRS

Writing this section would've been easy if erotic attraction and sexual behavior operated in a simple "yes, I'm very interested" or "no, I'm not interested at all" fashion. Then all we'd need to say would be that people having emotional affairs are in no way erotically invested in each other, while those involved in sexual affairs are going at it every moment they're together. But, of course, life is never that simple. The reality is that sometimes people are sexually attracted but don't act on their desires. Sometimes people aren't all that turned on but still find themselves in bed with each other. People sharing feelings might secretly lust for each other's body. People sharing their bodies with each other might really just want to talk. And sometimes it's hard to tell where a warm hug ends and a sensual caress begins.

Nevertheless, there's a world of difference between getting together mainly to share feelings and doing so with a more carnal purpose in mind. To demonstrate this point, just imagine a man and woman hugging each other as they meet in a park. First, picture them meeting to talk about their feelings. How do they touch? How do they smile? How do they look at each other? Now imagine them meeting for a sexual liaison. How do they touch? How do they smile? How do they look at each other? What differences do you see as you imagine these two scenes?

We define a sexual affair as an extramarital relationship between two people, primarily intended for sexual gratification. Perhaps these partners do share emotions from time to time, but that isn't mainly what brings them together.

Like emotional affairs, sexual affairs threaten the participants' commitment to their marriages or long-term relationships. They're the stuff of jealousy and soap operas.

TOTAL AFFAIRS

A "total affair" is our term for what happens when someone becomes involved with another person (outside his or her committed relationship or marriage) for both emotional and sexual reasons. This sounds beautifully romantic: "At last, I've met the man (or woman) of my dreams—my soul mate, my kindred spirit, the love of my life!" But then there are those nagging questions: "Now what am I going to do? Should I get a divorce? Or should I stick it out even though I don't really love my spouse? Will it last? What if it doesn't and I've given up everything for the sake of true love? Why do I feel so guilty? Why am I still hiding this relationship even from my best friends? Why am I so confused? Why do I feel paralyzed, unable to take a step in either direction?"

There's an answer to that last question, by the way. Lovers often feel paralyzed in their total affairs because they're, in effect, trying to compare apples to oranges. The apple, the committed relationship, offers the sweet and familiar taste of family, comfort, and routine; the orange, the affair, looks brighter and tastes sharper but tends to spoil easily. Even when someone is convinced she despises her partner, even when the two of them are sleeping in separate rooms, even when they're fighting night and day, still, home life maintains its gravitational pull. There's almost always an urge on the part of the participant involved in a total affair to break it off and head on home. If not, why do so many of these "made in heaven" matches end disastrously or gradually dribble off into nothingness?

Of course, total affairs are extremely threatening to a long-term relationship. The partner who was cheated on might easily feel doubly damaged, humiliated as both a sexual partner and a friend. Healing a marriage from a total affair takes a long time and a lot of effort.

Checklist: Is Your Partner Having an Emotional Affair?

We're assuming you're reading this book out of concern that your partner might be having an emotional affair. Probably there've been hints and signs that make you wonder what's going on. Maybe your partner spends more time away from home, just seems more distant, talks a lot about a particular individual, or makes up excuses to hide out in the computer room. Perhaps it's just a gut instinct on your part—you can't point to anything specific but still feel troubled and a little suspicious. Or maybe there isn't a whole lot of mystery, because your partner comes right out with something like, "You know, I like talking with _____ a lot more than talking with you." Another possibility is that things aren't going very well between the two of you and you're just looking for a possible explanation.

We've created a checklist to help you take stock of the situation. Completing the checklist will provide you with a general picture of the problem as well as pinpoint specific issues that need to be confronted.

However, before you begin working on the checklist, we want to issue several cautions. After all, you don't want to make the big mistake of accusing your partner of having an emotional affair if that's not what's happening. That will just create problems or make whatever's going wrong between you a lot worse. So don't begin until you've carefully read through these cautions.

Don't even think about completing the questionnaire if you're just looking for a weapon with which to attack your partner. "Ha! Now I've got you! You're having an emotional affair, aren't you? Don't tell me you're innocent, you stupid…" Be honest with yourself. If you're really angry right now at your partner and want to hurt him or her, back off. Wait until you've calmed down and can be more objective about what's happening in your relationship.

Give your partner the benefit of the doubt while looking through the checklist. We're not saying you should be naive or gullible. But the whole idea of a strong relationship centers on mutual trust. So trust until there's good reason not to trust.

Be aware of your own relationship insecurities. Are you prone to jealousy? Have you made unfounded accusations against your current partner or past partners? Do you have a pattern of looking for "proof" that your partner doesn't really love you or will eventually abandon you? If so, be very cautious when you review the checklist. You may be misreading this situation as you have done in the past.

Use the questionnaire for general information. Don't take your answers as absolute proof that your partner is having an emotional affair. We say this because this checklist has not been rigorously and scientifically validated. It's just a guide. Use it carefully as only one way to get a better picture of what's going on in your relationship.

Vague feelings or gut instincts aren't enough to indicate that your partner is having an emotional affair. Ask yourself this question before answering yes to any item: "Can I think of a specific occasion when I'm certain this particular event occurred?"

Don't make yourself paranoid by only searching for evidence that supports your claim. For example, perhaps your partner did just spend an evening having supper with his or her good friend. But don't forget that last week your partner turned down several invitations to go out in order to stay home with you. If you ignore disconfirming evidence, you can always prove your claim, but you won't be a very good detective.

One negative episode doesn't make a pattern. Try not to make too much out of any single incident that bothers you. An emotional affair only occurs when your partner has developed a distinct and lasting pattern of behaviors in which he or she directs emotional energy away from you and toward another.

Just because things aren't going well between you doesn't mean your partner is having an emotional affair. Perhaps your partner has been coming home late, sleeping downstairs, and leaving home early. That doesn't sound good. Something may be going wrong in your relationship. But just because he or she is avoiding you doesn't mean someone else is in the picture.

Remember, partners in a healthy relationship have the right to form friendships with others and spend some time apart. True, too much separation creates loneliness and a deep feeling that something is missing in the relationship. But too much closeness can feel smothering. The idea is to achieve a comfortable balance between time apart and time together.

There's an important difference between privacy and secrecy. A certain amount of personal privacy is natural and positive in a relationship, but secrecy creates problems. Privacy is about keeping something to oneself, not because it's bad but because it's personal. Examples might be your quiet prayers, deepest dreams, and need for time alone. We speak of someone's right to privacy because we know how important it is to experience solitude sometimes. Secrecy, on the other hand, is associated with guilt and shame. We keep secrets out of fear that others would disapprove of us if they discovered what we thought or did. Practically, this difference between privacy and secrecy is very important in distinguishing between friendships and emotional affairs. Your partner has a right to friendships. He or she even has the right to share some things with others and not with you. That's privacy. However, if two people meet on the sly, knowing full well that something questionable is going on between them, that's a secretive relationship. If these people also encourage each other to avoid their partners and instead talk only with them, that's more secretive than private. Emotional affairs are secretive relationships. But as you complete the checklist, remember to allow your partner the right to privacy.

Is Your Partner Having an Emotional Affair?

Please use the following key as you go through the list:

N: *I see no indication that my partner is acting or thinking this way.*

O: *Occasionally; I observe my partner acting like this about once every week.*

F: *Frequently; I see my partner acting this way several times a week.*

D: *Daily; my partner acts this way at least once a day.*

My partner...

_____ 1. ...is more likely to tell that friend what bothers him or her than to tell me.

_____ 2. ...chooses to have lunch or dinner with that friend instead of me.

_____ 3. ...talks about important things with that person rather than with me.

_____ 4. ...says this friend understands him or her better than I do.

_____ 5. ...says he or she perfectly understands this other person.

_____ 6. ...says it's as if the two of them can read each other's mind.

_____ 7. ...puts that friend on a pedestal as if he or she has no faults.

_____ 8. ...acts as if all his or her troubles vanish when that person is near.

_____ 9. ...says that this friend meets emotional needs that I cannot.

_____ 10. ...seems very attracted to him or her but denies any sexual interest.

_____ 11. ...gets angry or defensive when I ask him or her about that relationship.

_____ 12. ...doesn't even try to come to me to get his or her emotional needs met.

_____ 13. ...acts empty, lonely, or desperate when he or she can't contact that person.

_____ 14. ...apologizes or says he or she feels guilty about that relationship.

_____ 15. ...says that his or her other relationship feels special or really important.

_____ 16. ...ignores the concerns others have raised about his or her friendship with this person.

_____ 17. ...goes out of his or her way to spend time with this friend even if it interferes with events in our life or the opportunity for us to spend time together.

_____ 18. ...always seems to be thinking about the third party.

_____ 19. ...has mentioned having had thoughts of leaving me now that he or she has met this other person.

_____ 20. ...might deny it, but the phrase "emotional affair" just seems to fit my partner's relationship with that person.

Scoring:

For each letter in the key, give your partner the following number of points:

N = 0 points

O = 1 point

F = 2 points

D = 3 points

The total number of possible points is 60. (Remember, this checklist has not been scientifically validated. The interpretations we offer are meant as suggestions only.)

Suggested Interpretation:

0–9: Probably not much to worry about, but ask yourself if you could be minimizing.

10–19: These scores average out to less than 1 point per item, but they do suggest that your partner might be getting more involved than he or she realizes.

20–29: Your partner is involved in an outside relationship that's beginning to take a significant amount of time and energy away from your committed partnership.

30–45: Your partner is regularly engaged in an emotional relationship with someone else to the point that your committed relationship is seriously damaged.

46–60: Your partner is having a full-blown emotional affair that could destroy your committed relationship.

Now that you've read this chapter and completed the test, choose one of the following statements to describe what's happening and place a check mark beside it:

_____ I am absolutely convinced my partner is having an emotional affair.

_____ I think it's pretty likely my partner is having an emotional affair.

_____ It's certainly possible, but I just can't say at this time whether my partner is having an emotional affair.

_____ I don't think my partner is having an emotional affair, but it's possible.

_____ I'm certain my partner is not having an emotional affair.

NOW WHAT DO YOU DO?

Warning: don't do anything yet! Even if you're completely convinced your partner is having an emotional affair, don't take any drastic actions, such as angrily confronting your partner, kicking him or her out of the house, or taking out a restraining order against him or her. Above all, do not attack your partner physically or verbally. Give yourself at least a few days to observe some more, think about the situation, and calm down. This situation didn't develop overnight and therefore cannot be resolved immediately.

Read the rest of this book—slowly. Take time to notice how your partner's behavior has affected you. Then you'll be ready to consider how to approach the problem in a way that can do more good than harm.

2

How Your Partner's Emotional Affair Affects You

*P*ainful, stressful—these two words say it all when your partner is having an emotional affair. First, it just plain hurts to realize that the person you love is giving priority to someone other than you. Somehow you no longer come first in your partner's eyes, at least not in some very important ways. Sometimes the hurt may be like a dull pain, a low-intensity headache that you only notice when you think about it. But at other times the pain suddenly becomes more severe. That's when you can hardly bear to think about what's happening but can't stop thinking about it either. Perhaps your pain feels excruciating, so bad that you want to scream to God that this just can't keep going on or you'll go crazy.

Second, stress takes over. You don't sleep well. You feel anxious most of the time. Nothing seems easy and nothing goes well. You worry, worry, worry. Life is hard.

In this chapter we'll describe five main areas of your life that may be severely affected when your partner is having an emotional affair. Of course, people are different. You may be affected more strongly in one area than someone else is, but less potently in others. For example, if your thinking is fairly unaffected, you may only suffer from small distractions, such as having to endure moments of forgetfulness. On the other hand, if the impact is stronger, you might develop an almost complete inability to concentrate.

We'll begin with how your partner's emotional affair might affect your thinking. Most likely you'll experience moments of forgetfulness, distraction, and obsession.

What about your emotions? That's the second area for discussion. One emotional reaction, for instance, might be feelings of guilt over the thought that you should be a better partner. We're not saying that's right. In fact, it's not usually useful to have that kind of thought. But still, guilt is a very common emotional reaction to this problem.

Third, what's happening to your body? We'll discuss how people react to stress, especially the kind of grinding stress that occurs when the emotional affair goes on for a long time. It's difficult to take good care of yourself during such a slow-building crisis. But if you don't, the stress will keep getting worse.

Next, we need to inquire about your visible behavior, your words and actions. What are you doing that's good for you? What are you doing that might backfire badly (for example, following your partner to see if he or she is spending time with your rival)? What are you saying and to whom are you saying it? Are your actions helping you cope with this emotional affair, or are they just making things worse?

Finally, we hope you'll take a careful look at your spiritual self. How is your spirit holding up during these trying times? Do you have hope for your future? Do you believe you and your partner will get through this crisis? Or are you sinking into despair, depression, or bitterness? That's a terrible way to go. But perhaps the main reason you've picked up this book is to help yourself find ways to stay more optimistic. If so, we'll try to help you learn how to keep your faith in yourself, your partner, and the universe.

Before we begin, here are two notes of caution: (1) Many of the signs and symptoms we'll describe could occur because of other things going on in your mind, body, and life. For example, your partner's emotional affair could be a source of your headaches. But so could work troubles, problems with the kids, a physical condition, and so on. So be careful not to assume the worst. (2) We'll describe some pretty strong problems that people encounter. However, you might actually experience milder versions of these concerns. It's okay to be mildly or moderately upset about your situation. Even so, your partner's possible emotional affair is something that needs to be addressed before it becomes a worse problem for you.

THE THOUGHT COMPONENT: YOU'RE NOT CRAZY

The brain is a marvelous organ. That couple of pounds of white and gray matter lets us encounter a challenge and figure out what to do about it. It's never purely rational, of course. The brain's perceptions are always colored by our previous experiences, expectations, and assumptions. Still, most of the time we humans are pretty good at handling life's demands. We can even keep functioning quite well during moderately stressful times. Indeed, a modest amount of stress actually often helps us think more clearly so we can come up with good solutions to our problems.

However, too much stress screws up our brains big time. You know that all too well if you've ever panicked when you most needed to think:

"Should I take that job or keep looking? Think, think, think— I can't think, I'm too worried. I don't know what to do."

"Should I get that surgery or tell the doctor no? Think, think, think—I can't think. I'm too scared to think."

"Should I confront my husband about this emotional affair he's having? Think, think, think—I can't think. I'm so confused."

Here's our point: It's usually very stressful to be the partner of someone who's having an emotional affair. And that stress makes it hard to think well. Maybe you're experiencing some of the following symptoms.

Confusion

Your relationship certainly matters a lot to you. Otherwise you probably wouldn't be reading this book. And now that relationship is threatened by your partner's stupid friendship with someone else—a friendship, of all things, not even a sexual affair. At least if it were a sexual liaison, there'd be some cultural guidelines you could fall back on. You could be angry, hurt, indignant, jealous, or depressed, and people would understand your pain. But what do you do with this thing called an emotional affair? And when you talk to others, you don't get any consistent advice. One person says to ignore it. Another says to confront your partner. Your partner says it's not even happening, that it's all in your head. No wonder you're confused.

Denial

"Well, maybe it really isn't happening. Perhaps I'm imagining the whole thing. Just because she's spending several hours every day on the phone with him doesn't mean there's anything wrong. She says it's about business. Maybe I should believe her. Then why does her energy level fall as soon as she gets off the phone? Oh well, I'm probably just imagining that too."

People deny reality when they cannot handle it. Denial works to lessen pain. According to Robert Sapolsky, the brilliant researcher and writer about stress, denial can be very sensible if you're denying something that you can't change (2004, 415). Why think about it at all in that case? However, you certainly can do something here. You're not helpless. You need to break through your denial in order to confront the cause of your pain.

Minimization

To minimize is to make something appear smaller than it really is. So, if you're saying to yourself that your partner's emotional affair is really no big deal, you're probably minimizing. It *is* a big deal. You need to accept that fact so you can start doing something about it. Believe us, not many emotional affairs just go away if you ignore them.

Obsession

Now you can't stop thinking about it. You go over the details a thousand times in your mind. You cannot concentrate on anything else. Yes, you keep telling yourself to think about something else, anything else. But after a minute or two, your mind goes right back to the emotional affair. You're trapped in a mental prison.

Forgetfulness and Distraction

Your mental attention may focus so much on this one problem that you simply can't concentrate on anything else. That's when you can get seriously spacey. "When was that appointment? What appointment? Why was I going there? Where am I? Who am I?"

You may be experiencing some or all of these problems with your thinking. Maybe you're alternating between denial and obsession. The bottom line is that it's just plain difficult to think straight when your partner is having an emotional affair.

THE EMOTIONAL COMPONENT: FEELINGS ON OVERDRIVE

It's not only your reasoning ability that suffers when your partner is having an emotional affair. Chances are pretty good that you're experiencing some awfully weird feelings as well. If not, you might still be in the first phase of the crisis, where you've only just realized what's going on.

Numbness

Your initial reaction to the shock might be to go numb. Numbness is the emotional equivalent of denial. "This can't be happening, so I won't let myself feel anything. I'll just carry on as if everything is normal. I'll pretend to people that I'm feeling great. I won't even admit to myself that I feel bad." Going numb is a survival reaction that happens in situations where someone is overwhelmed by his or her initial reaction to a dangerous scene. Sometimes you have to turn off your feelings just to exist. But numbness can only last so long. Even though you don't consciously notice anything, almost certainly you're actually beginning to feel some pretty powerful emotions deep inside your soul. Sooner or later, they'll probably break loose. One at a time or in groups, in sudden bursts or slower waves, your emotions will refuse to stay in hiding. And when they do emerge, it'll be all you can handle to keep them in check.

Anger

Anger may be the first emotion to show up when your feelings break through. That's definitely not bad, because anger is our emotional system's best messenger when something goes wrong. Imagine receiving an e-mail like this: "Hey, what's going on over there? Can't you see that this is wrong? He doesn't have any right to be talking all day to that other woman. Who does he think he is? Stand up to him—right now. Tell him you won't put up with this garbage."

Be careful with your anger though. It's all too easy to explode at your partner, to say exactly the wrong things, to hurt your partner just for the sake of hurting him or her. You can push your partner away with your anger just when you want him or her to get close. So let yourself feel your anger. Listen very carefully to the messenger. But don't act hastily. Let things settle enough to where you can speak reasonably calmly with your partner. It's okay to stay angry though. You'll need that anger to help you act effectively.

Fear

Fear is a strong feeling that might vie with anger for your attention. "Oh my God, what's going to happen next? Is this the end of our relationship? Is she going to leave me?" Fear can make you call your partner ten times a day seeking reassurance that you're still loved. And strong fear seems to feed on itself. The more you notice your fear, the more scared you become. Eventually fear can become paralyzing. Just when you most need to say and do something may be when your fear keeps you pinned to the ground.

Nevertheless, you need your fear almost as much as you need anger. Fear reminds you of how important this relationship is to you. After all, if you didn't give a rip whether your partner cared, you wouldn't feel so scared. But you do need to deal with your fear. It may be helpful to share your fears with your partner, if he or she can deal with them. But we hope you also have others you trust who can help ease your fears. Being scared isn't something you need to go through alone.

Loneliness

The thought of going through life alone leads to another emotion: loneliness. Nobody enters into a serious relationship to feel lonely. We commit ourselves to another to feel deeply bonded. Life is simply better for most of us when we've found a partner. Unfortunately, emotional affairs are like acid that steadily drips upon this loving bond. Eventually connections are severed. Closeness surrenders to distance, and a special kind of loneliness emerges. Right when you should feel safe and warm in the caring arms of your partner, you actually feel empty, cold, and lonely.

By now you may have correctly surmised that we believe that every one of your emotions is important during this crisis. So what's the use for loneliness? Like fear, loneliness reminds you of how important this particular relationship is to you. It stokes the desire to reconnect, giving you more energy to work through your differences. But that's not all. Loneliness like this drives people toward others—friends, family, groups. It could even steer you toward taking a chance on another committed partnership if this one proves unsalvageable. But do be careful. We're not suggesting that you begin an affair of your own or develop a "backup" relationship so you won't feel lonely.

Sadness

Sadness may burrow deep into your heart when your partner becomes emotionally overinvolved with another. It's often triggered when people remember a more satisfying past. "She used to tell me everything important in her life. Now she never tells me anything. When I think about that, I want to cry." It's like watching a 100-watt lightbulb dim to about 25 watts and threaten to go out entirely. Sadness like this feels like grief. Indeed, you're grieving the loss of emotional closeness. Your sadness serves to remind you of how good your relationship once was and perhaps could be again.

But what if you add a feeling of hopelessness to your sadness? What happens if your partner won't break off the emotional affair? Or perhaps the affair ends, but the two of you can't seem to retrieve that wonderful sense of closeness? That's when you can develop serious depression. Probably, at first this will be what's called "situational" depression, which occurs when someone's body and brain slow way down in response to a long-lasting, serious problem that has begun to feel unfixable. But situational depression sometimes triggers more-serious biological depression. Now the brain doesn't make enough chemicals called *neurotransmitters* (especially *serotonin*), and you're really in trouble. You should consult a counselor or doctor if you think you might be depressed.

Disgust

Here's another emotion you may be feeling: disgust. "I used to be so attracted to him. But now I feel a wave of revulsion when he comes into the room. I can't even stand looking at him." You'll know it's disgust if you feel like turning away from your partner as if he or she were ugly, dirty, or spoiled. Disgust is a primary emotion, initially developed so that we'd instinctively turn up our noses at rotten food or spit out contaminated water. But over tens of thousands of years, that sense of disgust has been recruited for social purposes. Now we turn away in disgust from noxious social stimuli just as we do from bad food.

You may also hold in contempt the rival with whom your partner has connected. "That pig, that loser, that moron—I don't see why anyone would want to talk to him. I can't respect him. And, if she's that involved with him, then I don't respect her either."

Disgust sends a distinct and simple message: "Man, this whole situation stinks." It's time to either clean up the mess or get out.

Guilt

Now let's talk about guilt. Perhaps you believe that you must be doing something wrong. Maybe you're too bossy, distant, needy, angry, nosy, mean, distracted, tired, or busy. You must be too "something" to deserve this fate. Certainly your partner would like you to take the blame. "It's your fault. You're driving me away because you're too bossy, too distant..." Of course, you need to study your actions. And if you can make some positive changes, great. But whatever you say and do, whoever you are, you're not the person choosing to have an emotional affair. That guilt belongs to your partner, not you.

Shame

Finally, what about shame? Shame is when you feel that there's something really wrong with you. Shame comes in five varieties, what we call "deficiency messages": *I'm not good, I'm not good enough, I'm unlovable, I don't belong, I shouldn't even exist* (Potter-Efron 1989, 76). Every one of these deficiency messages can get worse when your partner develops an emotional affair. How can you feel good about yourself when your partner's actions seem to imply all of these shameful things about you? It's hard not to believe that there must be something that makes you unattractive to your partner. Self-esteem almost invariably suffers.

Shame feels horrible. It makes you want to hide, to hang your head. But even shame has its value, as long as it doesn't last too long. Right now, as you read this book, your shame may help you realize that your partner's emotional affair is dragging you down. However, by the time you're done dealing with this situation, perhaps you'll remember what it feels like to hold your head up high.

THE PHYSICAL COMPONENT: HEARTACHES AND HEADACHES

As we've seen, trying to deal with your partner's emotional affair is mentally and emotionally exhausting. It's usually hard on your body as well. That's especially true if the affair goes on and on. There's a lot of research on the negative effects of long-term stress on your body. Basically, the problem is that we humans are better designed to deal with short-lived crises than with longer ones. Let's say you and your partner Sal head out to have a little fun at the local tavern. Ten minutes after you arrive, you notice some drunken fool hitting on Sal. Emergency! Emergency! Immediately (actually, usually within less than a second) your faithful brain gives orders to prepare for a fight. Epinephrine (adrenaline) squirts into your bloodstream. Blood flows into your arms and legs so you can fight or flee. Your pulse rate soars. You feel totally agitated. And off you go, marching over to get between Sal and your newfound rival. Five minutes later, it's all over. Your rival has been dispatched to the other side of the bar, Sal is back in your arms, and you already feel yourself relaxing. The danger is over. You body returns to normal. That's the kind of stress our bodies are well prepared to handle.

Now compare that scene with what happens between you and your partner during an emotional affair. First off, your rival may be unseen and virtually unknown to you. There goes the possibility of that scary but rewarding frontal confrontation. Second, it's not nearly as clear exactly what danger you face. This isn't someone trying to wrestle your lover out of your grasp. No, it's "only" someone who spends a lot of time sharing emotions and experiences with your partner. This feels more like shadowboxing than a real fight. Third, and most significant, few emotional affairs only last a few hours or days. It's quite the opposite. All too often they last weeks, months, even years. And as they linger, emotional affairs generate a seemingly endless number of painful encounters. Dealing with your partner's emotional affair becomes more like running a marathon than a sprint. But that's a serious problem for your body. It's probable that as long as the affair lasts, your body will stay on semi-alert status, like a soldier on guard duty in a hostile land, guarding the perimeter of the unit's territory. Maybe you won't be pumped full of adrenaline, but you won't really be at rest either. You'll be in a state of long-term stress. But how many serious discussions, arguments, "misunderstandings," and outright lies can you endure before your body starts to break down?

Long-term stress eats away at the most vulnerable places in your body. Here are some of the most common ways that your partner's emotional affair (and your attempts to cope with it) might be affecting you.

Sleep Problems

People whose partners are having emotional affairs may develop several sleep problems, including difficulty getting to sleep, staying asleep long enough (at least four hours) to complete the four phases of the sleep cycle, and returning to sleep if they awaken. Another problem is not actually feeling rested when you arise. How can you get a decent night's sleep when you can't quit worrying?

Muscle Aches and Pains

It's hard to really relax when you've become chronically stressed. That lack of relaxation keeps muscles tensed enough to create aches and pains. Sometimes these pains have obvious causes. At other times you just might feel sore all over. That's the kind of pain that drives doctors crazy, because they can't locate its source.

Headaches

Perhaps one of those chronically tense areas is in your shoulders or neck. Voila! Here comes that nagging headache you just can't seem to get rid of, the one that keeps coming back right after you've had yet another frustrating talk with your partner.

Vulnerability to Illness

Once, you were strong as a horse and seldom became ill. Now you wonder if you've developed allergies or whether there's mold in the house or if something else strange is going on. Stress tends to make people more prone to illness and disease. Certainly the stress of dealing with your partner's emotional affair might make you more vulnerable to illness.

Sexual Desire Problems

Human beings have interesting sexual mechanisms, because a seeming paradox exists at the center of our eroticism. In general, both men and women need to feel safe and relaxed to become erotically aroused. Unfortunately, "safe and relaxed" doesn't exactly describe the affective state of someone whose partner is indulging in an emotional affair. "Unsafe and tense" is more accurate. No wonder, then, that sexual interactions become less frequent and less satisfying.

BEHAVIORAL PROBLEMS: WHEN YOU CAN'T DO ANYTHING RIGHT

Okay, here's where we are so far. Your brain's not working very well. Your emotions are out of whack. Your body's a wreck. So how do you think all this will affect your behavior? Panicky minds trigger impulsive actions. Intense feelings produce troublesome overreactions. And all of this gets worse if you're too sleep deprived, headachy, or ill to make decent decisions. So then you say and do thoughtless things that only make the situation worse. And that makes it easy for your partner to blame everything on you: "Well, if you weren't so crazy, I wouldn't need another friend. I can't talk with you. It's your fault."

Here are several unhelpful actions the partners of people who are having emotional affairs are prone to take.

Trying to Please

Some try desperately to please their partners, hoping that, by being really nice, they can win them back. The trouble is you may end up doing more of exactly the things your partner dislikes in the first place. For example, a man named Herm never quite figured out that his wife Shelley disliked flowers. So when she began her emotional affair, Herm went out and bought her several bouquets. That just told Shelley he'd never understand her as her new friend did.

Turning Away

Others turn away from their partners with a "You can't fire me, because I quit!" mentality. They become irate, disgusted, and even vengeful. They want to hurt their partners, to make them pay. Sometimes we see these wounded souls in marriage counseling. Unfortunately, they spend most of their time (at least at the start of therapy) blaming, shaming, and attacking their partners. That, of course, is not a very good way to encourage your partner to come back to you emotionally.

Indulging in Jealousy

Intense jealousy is another common problem in this situation. "Where are you going? Are you going to talk with her? Why won't you talk with me instead? Don't you love me? Don't you care? Is that her on the phone? Hang up now! Hang up! What are you thinking? Are you thinking about her? Can't we spend the whole weekend together? Was that her in the blue sedan that just went by the house? Did you see her today at work? No? I don't believe you!" And sometimes it's not just words. Anxious partners listen in on phone calls, dissect computer logs, follow their partners around, repeatedly ask others what they know, and contact their rivals to threaten them.

None of these actions help much, although they may let you feel a little more in control. They frequently backfire, as when your partner comes home to angrily protest that nasty call you made to his or her friend.

Using Mood-Altering Substances and Behaviors

Mood-altering substances and compulsive, mood-altering behaviors are two things that you need to be especially careful to avoid or minimize at this time. Right now you may be hurting both emotionally and physically. You're human, so you want relief. But be careful. Watch your intake of alcohol, nicotine, caffeine, prescribed pain medications, and "informal" pain relievers, such as marijuana and cocaine. It would be all too easy to become increasingly dependent on these substances instead of tackling the problem head on. For that matter, be cautious about how much shopping, gambling, or even working you do. It's easy for people to become compulsive about these kinds of behaviors, which can allow them to hide from their painful reality for a short while. Meanwhile, your reality will probably keep getting worse.

THE SPIRITUAL COMPONENT: LOSING HOPE

Janice realized months ago that her husband Barry was spending a lot of time with their mutual friend Sondra. She confronted him about it right away. Barry immediately became righteously indignant. "Are you accusing me of having an affair?" he demanded. Barry insisted he'd never, ever betray their marriage. So Janice backed off even though she still felt that something was wrong.

After that conversation, the pattern became predictable. If Janice so much as asked where he was going, Barry became defensive and angry. Janice tried to explain that she believed Barry wasn't having a romantic liaison with Sondra. She just questioned his literally spending hours at a time with Sondra while seldom making time for her.

No matter what she said though, he refused to honor her concerns. He just wouldn't listen, much less change his behavior. Eventually Janice felt as if she had become mired in emotional quicksand. The more she struggled, the more stuck she felt. Then, slowly she quit struggling.

Lately Janice has been feeling blue. Normally she's energetic, optimistic, positive, and playful. But now there are days when she feels tired, pessimistic, and way too serious. Life is getting hard. There seem to be more bad days than good. People have always called Janice a fighter, but now she's pretty much given up the fight. "Why bother?" she asks. "I can't make him listen. All we do is argue when I bring up his relationship with Sondra. What's the point?" So now Janice and Barry spend their "together" time emotionally apart. Sure, they sometimes talk about the weather, the kids, the economy—safe topics that won't lead to a fight. Still, there's that big elephant in the living room they both try to ignore.

You're probably thinking that Janice sounds depressed. That's definitely true, but she might use other words to convey what she feels: despairing, defeated, hopeless, indifferent. That word "hopeless" is critical. Janice feels as if she's lost her best friend and can't get him back. She has begun to believe that her marriage will never be emotionally intimate again. So now she's pulling back, spending less time and energy on the marriage.

Janice feels resentful too. She never thought she could get so angry and frustrated with her husband. But this emotional affair has gone on for months with no end in sight. It keeps eating at her all day. Plus, she deeply resents Sondra for ruining their friendship by becoming so involved with Barry. Now these two women barely talk with each other. They've become rivals instead of friends.

You feel resentful when someone keeps doing something bad to you that he or she could, but won't, stop. However, resentment doesn't represent the end of the line for long-term anger. Unhealed resentment can turn into hatred. In a previous work, we defined hatred as "an intense, unending loathing" of someone (Potter-Efron 2006, 169). You hate someone when you cannot and will not forgive her for her trespasses against you. Most relationships fail once someone views his or her partner with contempt. By then, all you see is how bad, even evil, your partner is. Fortunately, Janice hasn't gotten there yet, but she, like many people whose partners are having emotional affairs, is moving in that direction.

It's bad enough that Janice feels hopeless and resentful. She also feels very bitter. They spent all these years together for what? So that Barry could pour his heart out to another woman? "How is that fair? How can that be right?" Janice senses herself shriveling up inside like a raisin in the sun. And that scares her. Not only is she losing Barry, she's losing herself. What's happened to her capacity for joy? It's disappeared into the fog of her troubled marriage, along with her spontaneity and sense of humor. Life has become dull and ugly. Trouble is, the more Janice ponders her fate, the more bitter she feels. Lately she's been on the Internet looking for one of those old bumper stickers: "Life sucks and then you die."

Janice has become deeply dispirited. Dictionary synonyms for the word "dispirited" include discouraged, dejected, disheartened, and gloomy. Those are powerful words. But it's the "spirit" part of the word that is most important here. People need to feel a kind of good faith in their relationships. It's important to believe that both partners are working together hand in hand, helping each other survive and thrive. Emotional affairs disrupt that connection. Now, instead of walking and working in unison, they've separated. Emotional affairs produce an intimate disconnection that damages both heart and soul.

Checklist: How Has Your Partner's Emotional Affair Affected You?

This checklist will help you recognize how your partner's emotional affair has affected you. But, just as we did in the last chapter, we ask you to be careful not to exaggerate or overemphasize. For example, maybe you feel depressed but always do at this time of year. That wouldn't count for these purposes. On the other hand, perhaps you always get a little depressed about now, but it's a lot worse this year, especially since you realized what's going on. That almost surely is a sign that your partner's emotional affair is significantly affecting you. Try to take the middle ground between attributing too much or too little importance to the emotional affair.

Possible Effects of Your Partner's Emotional Affair on You

Cognitive Effects:

_____ Confusion

_____ Denial

_____ Minimization

_____ Obsession

_____ Forgetfulness and distraction

_____ Other (describe) _____

Emotional Effects:

_____ Numbness

_____ Anger

_____ Fear

_____ Loneliness

_____ Sadness

_____ Disgust

_____ Guilt

_____ Shame

_____ Other (describe) _____

Physical Effects:

_____ Sleep problems

_____ Aches and pains

_____ Stomach problems

_____ Headaches

_____ More colds, flus, and so on

_____ Sexual disinterest

_____ Other (describe) _____

Behavioral Effects:

_____ Trying too hard to please your partner

_____ Turning away from your partner

_____ Being intensely jealous

_____ Using mood-altering substances

_____ Developing compulsive (repetitive) behaviors

_____ Detective work (listening in on or recording calls, hacking into your partner's files, following your partner, and so on)

_____ Other (describe) _____

Spiritual Effects:

_____ Feelings of hopelessness

_____ Resentment toward your partner or his or her friend

_____ Bitterness

_____ Feeling generally dispirited

_____ Other (describe) _____

How do you think you've been affected the most as a result of your partner's emotional affair? _____

_____

Overall, have the effects so far been: _____ mild, _____ significant, or _____ strong?

What could you do immediately that might lessen the effects your partner's emotional affair is having upon you? _____

_____

(Note: See the next exercise for some ideas that might help you to quickly feel better.)

Your Survival Kit

You've just taken a look at how your partner's emotional affair has affected you. That's a good start. But just checking off items on a list won't help you get better. You need to find ways to take care of yourself when you feel blue, tired, anguished, scattered, or hurt. We've developed a survival kit that will help you be kind to yourself during this difficult time. It's as varied as a first-aid kit, full of ideas from which you can select. Everything on the list is something that you have the power to do to make yourself feel better. Instead of going numb, falling apart, or indulging in compulsive behaviors, use these suggestions to help get you grounded.

- Get to bed early enough to get a full night's sleep. Prepare for sleep by creating a period of physical and mental calmness. Perhaps a cup of chamomile tea would be just the right thing for you, or a gentle book, or maybe simply taking some alone time before bed would be helpful. If sleep continues to be problematic, consult a doctor.

- What about eating? Think moderation here: don't skip meals and don't overindulge. Keep reasonable amounts of food items you can use for quick energy. And don't try to self-medicate by overeating or eating a lot of sweets and other unhelpful carbohydrates.

- Exercise in moderation. Aerobic exercise is good for your heart. Count any exercise you get; a pedometer will help you keep track of the fact that you exercise every day, even if you're unaware of it. Or take a class, so you're doing something with others.

- Call or visit a friend. Choose someone who won't tell you what to do but will support you as you decipher your thoughts and feelings.

- Take a bath, shower, or swim. Relax in the water.

- Put on music and dance by yourself until you feel that your feet are back on the ground.

- Pretend you're your favorite kind of tree by sitting in a chair and imagining that your tailbone extends down into a root that goes right through everything, deep into the earth. Let your breathing change as you sit for a while, grounded, rooted, and beautiful.

- Getting involved in a hobby or pursuing one you already have will lessen obsession by giving you something interesting to think about.

- Try a Bach flower remedy called "Rescue Remedy" or make a cup of relaxing tea or hot chocolate, and sip it slowly. Remember that all human beings are connected and that you are perfectly human.

- If you're busy judging yourself because you believe your partner's emotional affair must be your fault, talk back to the judge you carry around in your head. If you absolutely can't get rid of your guilt, consider checking with a counselor or physician to see if you might be depressed.

- Sometimes people take their anger and frustration with others out on themselves. If you're seriously upset and find yourself tempted to harm yourself by "accidentally" burning yourself on a pot, cutting yourself, making yourself throw up, or scratching yourself raw, use a hotline, a very good friend, or a counselor to help you stop turning your anger on yourself.

- If you can't stop being angry with your partner and feel tempted to hurt him or her, remind yourself that being vengeful won't do much good. Try to figure out an appropriate thing for you to do instead of hurting your partner back. You may want to consider how to become more accepting, and even forgiving, of your partner.

- Watch funny movies. Make yourself laugh. Nothing is better for the soul than a good laugh.

- Read a good book or listen to your favorite music (but avoid sad songs).

- Help someone else. Sometimes helping others can put your problems in a better perspective.

- Find an old or broken item, take it home, and fix it.

- Choose a favorite blanket and use it.

As you can see, a survival kit can contain many things. Choose the ones you really need and will actually use. Doing something for yourself every day will make you stronger, since you won't always feel sad and victimized. It will keep you in better shape to talk about these problems with your partner when possible and to find helpers to support you.

3

Why Would My Partner Have an Emotional Affair?

$\mathcal{W}$e discussed one huge question during the first two chapters of this book: Is this really happening? Is your partner really having an emotional affair? You might have answered that question with: "Yes, I'm certain," "Maybe, I'm just not sure," or "Thank goodness, I don't think so."

Now, in this chapter we plan to address the next most important question you're probably asking yourself: "Why is my partner having an emotional affair?" We'll look at many possible answers to that question. But as we do, please keep several thoughts in mind:

■ We'll discuss the person who's having the emotional affair, but the information is intended for you, to help you better understand what's happening. The more you comprehend what's going on, the better able you'll be to figure out what to do about it.

■ The goal of asking why is to gather information that will help you and your partner recover from the emotional affair. It isn't to blame or shame either of you.

- However, your partner may try to blame you for his or her emotional affair. For example: "You aren't loving enough." "You're too demanding." "You're too critical." "You don't give me enough attention." *Just because your partner says these things doesn't make them true.* You'll need to give serious thought to your behavior, of course, as you try to recover your relationship. But don't begin from the assumption that there must be something seriously wrong with you. Make a mental note that we'll tackle the painful questions, "Is it my fault?" and "Am I doing something wrong?" in chapter 4.

- *Why* is a very difficult question to answer. Don't expect to find one simple reason in the complex world of human relationships. Be prepared for partial answers, vague responses, and frustration.

- Your partner might not know why this is happening, at least when you first discuss it together. That's okay for starters but not for the long term. Eventually your partner will need to take full responsibility for his or her actions. That includes owning up to the issue of why he or she began or continued the emotional affair.

- Your partner could have several different reasons, all of which will be important to discuss. Try to handle them one at a time so you don't get overwhelmed.

THE "I WANT..." AGENDA OF THE STRAYER

Here's our format for the rest of this chapter. We'll start from the belief that partners engaging in emotional affairs want something that's emotionally important to them. For instance, your partner might say that she wants love, respect, attention, or friendship. She may very well add a word that compares her emotional affair with her relationship with you. That word is "more," as in "I want more love, respect, attention, or friendship" than she receives from you. Sometimes the word may be "less," as in "I want less criticism, negativity, demands, or closeness." After all, it's hard to justify having an emotional affair if your partner perfectly meets your every need. Who wants to say that he or she's doing this merely out of greediness, self-centeredness, or boredom?

You'll need a lot of courage to face these accusations. But remember what we said a minute ago: just because your partner says these things doesn't make them true. On the other hand, just because your partner says these things doesn't make them false either. You'll really need to think carefully about everything your partner says are the reasons for the emotional affair, especially when you hear those "more" and "less" comparisons. Don't reject them out of hand. Don't swallow them whole. Do look for possible grains of truth in your partner's remarks even if you don't buy the whole story.

One more thing before you begin: as you read through these complaints, you might notice that you have an "I want more..." list of your own. That's only fair and reasonable. Eventually you'll both need to attend to each other's list of complaints so that you can heal your relationship.

More Emotional Connection

"I can never share my feelings with my partner. But I can, and do, with _____."

"I've always wanted someone with whom I could share everything."

"I never knew what it meant to feel really close to someone until I met _____."

In our work with partners engaged in emotional affairs, we've heard these three statements many times. They say they've found someone with whom they feel deeply emotionally connected. Perhaps this comes as a total surprise to them because they've never experienced true emotional intimacy with anyone before. Or maybe they once felt that powerful, warm connection with their partners, but too many arguments, stresses, and misunderstandings have eroded the quality of their relationships.

Your partner may have felt blocked from having or sharing feelings since childhood. After all, many children grow up in homes where they're told frequently not to feel anything at all, not to feel specific emotions ("Girls shouldn't get angry" or "Boys shouldn't be scared"), or not to express their emotions too strongly ("No matter what, keep your cool"). Now here comes a third party, Bob or Sally, saying that it's okay with him or her for your partner to be emotional. There's an emotional intensity to the relationship that's partly increased by its secretiveness.

It's usually far easier for the couple involved in the emotional affair than the committed partners to focus upon their emotional connection. They aren't paying the bills together, schlepping the kids to yet another dance concert, putting in mandatory overtime at work, or caring for elderly parents on the weekend. All that stress is the fodder that continually provides food for the emotional affair: "Could you get away for an hour tonight? I've got to talk to you about the kids. I need to share my feelings with you. No, I can't talk to my wife. She wouldn't understand." So the two involved in the emotional affair manage an hour together, taking away yet another opportunity to share their feelings with their committed partners.

What does this mean to you? First, ask yourself if this material is ringing any bells. Could this be one of the reasons your partner is having an emotional affair? If so, consider ways to invite him or her to share those emotions with you. But don't rush into anything just yet. Keep reading to see how many other reasons strayers claim for having an emotional affair might be relevant to your relationship.

More Understanding

"My partner doesn't understand me, but _____ does."

"It's as if _____ knows what I'm thinking before I even say it."

"It's not just that _____ understands me. I just know exactly what she (or he) means when she (or he) talks to me."

Emotional connections stand at the center of an emotional affair, of course. But sometimes people feel emotionally bonded by sharing ideas, opinions, and goals. Who of us hasn't thrilled when someone we're talking with nods his or her head vigorously and says, "Yes, I understand. That makes so much sense. I agree with you completely." This sense of mutual understanding can be as gratifying for some people as sex. Experiences like this might lead someone to create a belief that there's one and only one person who truly understands him or her. Needless to say, that leaves you out if you're not your partner's intellectual confidant.

Could this be one of the reasons your partner is having an emotional affair? Eventually you'll need to ask him or her to find out. Right now, let's keep your partner out of the picture. Instead, answer these questions:

When was the last time you and your partner really talked about important ideas?

Can you two discuss your life goals without getting into useless arguments?

Do you even know what thoughts, ideas, or opinions are most critical to your partner?

More Praise and Less Criticism

"My boyfriend takes me for granted. He never shows me any appreciation."

"All my wife does is criticize, criticize, criticize."

"My spouse tells me what I do wrong. My friend tells me what I do right."

Most couples we see in marriage counseling have forgotten how to praise each other. Instead, they spend countless hours criticizing, attacking, and generally bad-mouthing each other. The inevitable result is that they become defensive around each other, perhaps refusing to talk at all, only speaking about totally safe subjects or eagerly picking apart each other's comments to find fault. This very destructive behavior turns friends into enemies. So in counseling, we always ask partners to stop criticizing and start praising each other.

There's a kicker in this discussion though: you can praise your partner a hundred times a day, but it'll be useless if he or she can't, or won't, take in your comments. For example, imagine how someone could respond to this attempt at praise: "You sure did that fast." "Well, thanks, I'm glad you noticed" would be a nice and expected response. But think about these: "Are you saying I'm usually slow?" "You idiot! It's not speed that counts, it's accuracy" or "I hate it when you watch everything I do. Leave me alone!" Obviously, it takes two for praise to work, one praise giver and one receiver. If, for any reason, your partner has decided that you are a criticizer, not a praiser, he or she may ignore your attempts at appreciation or even hear them as criticisms. You'll end up thinking that you can never say anything right, no matter how hard you try. Along those same lines, your partner may believe you're criticizing him or her endlessly when you have no intention of doing so.

People who believe they get too little praise and too much criticism are like beautiful flowers in a deserted field. They need someone to come by and appreciate them. And if that someone wants to pick them up and take them home, well, maybe they'll go along with that idea.

Please note that the problem of insufficient praise and excess criticism often goes both ways. Neither person gives enough praise, not just the abandoned partner. Also, things may get worse when one partner wanders into an emotional affair. Now there are more reasons to criticize each other and fewer opportunities for praise. That makes the straying partner even hungrier for acceptance and appreciation. So whom will your partner turn to for that praise? Naturally, to the new friend.

Could this be a partial explanation for why your partner is having an emotional affair? Does your partner complain a lot about your alleged lack of appreciation of what he or she does or says?

How much does your partner desire praise or resent criticism? Some people need amazingly little praise. Most people need to hear regularly that they're really appreciated. And some people are like that proverbial bucket with a hole in it. They can simply never get enough praise, so they seek it constantly from everybody around them. The more your partner is like that, the more likely he or she will get involved in an emotional affair to get praise.

How sensitive is your partner to criticism? Some individuals are supersensitive. They hate even small criticisms (such as "Honey, please remember to put the cap back on the toothpaste container"). The more oversensitive your partner is to criticism, the more likely he or she will treasure a friend who's never critical. Real long-term relationships, of course, cannot be totally free of negativity and criticism. But someone having an emotional affair often compares the apple (the committed relationship) to the orange (the emotional affair). The strayer may fantasize that ending the committed relationship would allow him or her to live happily ever after with the emotional affair partner with never a smidgen of criticism.

More Freedom

"I feel smothered, like I can't even breathe."

"I need more space to be me, and my friend lets me do that."

"The kids, my job, money pressures—I need someone I can relax with."

It could be a twenty-five-year-old man who chafes at having to settle down with wife and family. Perhaps it's a forty-year-old woman whose teenage kids are more than she can stand. It could be a forty-five-year-old male whose partner keeps pushing him for emotional closeness when all he wants to do is get away. Then there's the fifty-year-old lady whose jealous partner falsely accuses her of carrying on a sexual affair. How about the sixty-year-old guy complaining that he's just plain tired of a lifetime of responsibilities? These people share a common theme. They all feel trapped. They struggle, sometimes quietly and sometimes loudly, against the chains of a committed relationship. They feel strongly that being in a committed relationship is too demanding, too time consuming, too energy draining, and too much work.

These individuals frequently build up lingering resentments against their committed partners. They hold their partners responsible for their obligations. If it weren't for those demanding partners, they could stay out later at night. They could get away from their kids. They could have a peaceful evening without another of those endless discussions about their feelings. They could quit their jobs right now, instead of having to endure another ten years until retirement. They could find a few minutes of peace without someone always asking questions about where they've been and what they've done. They hate the guilty feelings they experience when they think about evading their responsibilities. But instead of lessening their guilt by accepting their obligations, they blame their partners for their own bad feelings.

This isn't fair. Unhappy strayers essentially blame their committed partners for the very responsibilities and obligations they entered into voluntarily. They may not exactly say this out loud, or even to themselves, but these deeply resentful partners may secretly look for ways to evade their responsibilities or punish their partners. Getting involved in an emotional affair does both jobs quite nicely.

"Now that's not fair!" the straying partner might argue. "I just want a few moments of peacefulness. I'm not shirking my responsibilities." Sure. Tell that to your partner, who gradually spends more and more time alone while you are physically, mentally, and emotionally distant.

Could your partner be having an emotional affair at least partly as a protest against his or her obligations and responsibilities?

Does your partner complain a lot about how much he or she has to do around home, at work, and so on?

Is your partner someone who "suffers" silently while gradually becoming more and more resentful?

Does guilt get passed around your home like a hot potato?

Do you get told that it's your fault your partner has so many commitments in life, especially commitments to you?

More Action

"I'm kinda bored with _____ [my committed partner]. We never do anything new."

"Getting to know my friend is really exciting."

"I get high just sharing my feelings with my friend."

Almost all long-term relationships blend together a mixture of novelty and familiarity. Novelty comes in the form of spontaneous changes of plans, unexpected gifts, new ideas for the future, experimental ways to make love, and the unpredictability of life. And novelty doesn't necessarily wear out over time. Imagine a man celebrating his fiftieth anniversary, who says of his wife, "She still surprises me. I don't think I'll ever really know all about her." That statement is testimony to the value of unpredictability in every relationship.

Too much novelty, however, threatens the stability of committed relationships. Life becomes anxious when you never know what's going to happen next. Not many people want to live in a soap opera—like marriages featuring such lines as "But you said you'd be home by midnight!" and "No, I have no idea when I'll be home for supper. Or if I'll be home at all." Novelty, when not balanced with predictability, feels chaotic.

Predictability, the counterweight to novelty, can be a major benefit of living in a committed relationship. You know your partner will be there at the end of the day. You build in routines that make everything from making breakfast to making love less chancy. Grocery shopping doesn't call for a major conference, because you both know what each prefers. Life flows along efficiently based on normal and reliable patterns of behavior.

Too much predictability, however, is no better than too much novelty. It's not exactly stimulating to have the same conversations while consuming the same meals while watching the same television shows and then making love in precisely the same manner at 10 A.M. every other Saturday. Boredom sets in when predictability squeezes out novelty in a relationship.

Life demands balance. Hopefully, the dramatic music of novelty keeps playing in your committed relationship along with the harmony of the steadier second part, predictability. That means you've achieved a good working balance between these two important forces.

It's certainly possible that partners might develop emotional affairs if they felt that their committed relationships were too unpredictable and chaotic. Those individuals would value outsiders for their steadiness, reliability, and (paradoxically) loyalty. The special friend would probably be the kind of person who is "always there when I need someone to talk with." Together, they would develop safe and comfortable routines, exactly the patterns the straying partner feels are missing in his or her committed relationship. The committed relationship would suffer more then, because the strayer would quit trying as hard to get his or her need for predictability met within the partnership.

However, we hear more people engaged in emotional affairs say that they're simply bored with their lives. They seek more excitement, which they define as doing new things, discussing new ideas, sharing new emotions, and meeting new people. In short, they want more action. Getting heavily involved with someone new certainly is exciting. That's doubly true if the new person offers a whole range of new ideas, new things to do, and new ways to behave. And, once again, the straying partner damages the committed relationship. Instead of fighting to make that relationship more interesting, he or she transfers energy into the emotional affair. That's where all the action is. That's where the strayer wants to be.

Here are a few questions that might clarify how much your partner's emotional affair is triggered by the desire for more action:

Does your partner complain that nothing ever happens in your relationship?

Is your partner always eager to do something new?

What about you? Do you find your committed relationship a little too predictable?

More Emotional Intensity

"We seldom talk about anything important anymore."

"I'm someone who likes strong feelings. They're part of me. My friend brings them out."

"My marriage feels emotionally dead to me. I can't even get mad about it any more."

A dissatisfied partner may yearn for a level of emotional intensity that has gone missing from the committed relationship. If so, he or she will complain that the committed relationship is too placid. This individual wants more intense emotional involvement and stronger emotional expression. "Sure, we talk a lot. We even share our feelings a little—but nothing deep, nothing powerful, nothing really personal. It's as if we can be a little sad together, a little happy. But that's all. We never share deep feelings anymore. We don't even argue."

People differ in the extent to which they want to experience strong emotions. Powerful feelings are a turn-on to some, a turn-off to others. For every individual whose goal in life is to feel calm all day long, there's another who wants a daily lightning bolt of emotionality. Heart-wrenching sadness, elevating joy, terrifying fear, jaw-tightening anger—they're all anathema to some while providing the very meaning of life to others.

Let's focus for a minute on the latter group, the people who really yearn for strong emotions. One key to understanding them is to recognize their need for emotional intensity. These individuals feel most alive when awash in a sea of powerful emotions. Their lives tend to be dramatic, because they seek ways to generate the emotional equivalent of thunderous rainstorms (if not tornadoes) every day. You might say these people get high on their strong emotions.

Now imagine what might happen if an intense emotion–seeking individual pairs up with someone far less excited about living life one drama at a time. Maybe during courtship, this difference didn't register in their minds. After all, courtship is usually a time of strong emotions for both parties. But then the relationship begins to settle down. "Good," says one partner, "I've had plenty of excitement for a while." "Nuts," says the emotional-intensity fan, "where have all the feelings gone?" Dissatisfaction creeps in. The emotional-intensity seeker is left with thoughts such as, "Is this all there is? Is this all there's going to be?" That's when he or she starts looking for someone to rekindle those strong emotions. It'll probably be someone who also likes to feel intense emotions.

Furthermore, let's remember that emotional affairs usually have an element of secrecy. The simple act of hiding the full truth from the committed partner can raise the emotional stakes considerably. Risk-taking raises a person's anxiety level, something that the emotional-intensity seeker will complain about but also enjoy. But what if he or she eventually does get confronted by the committed partner? That's not all bad either since conflict raises the intensity level of that relationship as well. True, the straying partner may feel dizzying waves of guilt as he or she realizes the extent of the damage done, but even that guilt at least helps him or her feel fully alive. The greater problem comes when the straying partner considers ending the emotional affair. How would he or she feed that internal demand for intense feelings then? Life might get dull again.

Is your straying partner's craving for powerful emotional experiences fueling the emotional affair? Ponder these questions:

Does your partner talk about a desire to experience strong emotions?

Does it seem as if your partner almost encourages conflict over what he or she is doing?

Do you prefer considerably less emotional intensity than your partner?

More Respect

"My boyfriend doesn't even listen to me when I talk to him."

"She interrupts me all the time. It's as if my ideas aren't important."

"My partner never takes my wants and needs into consideration."

Feeling respected is something almost everybody values. It's a way for others to tell us that we're important enough to be seen, heard, and taken seriously. Furthermore, mutual respect is expected in our American, democratic relationships. Being respectful is a way of honoring one's partner within intimate relationships.

It's not all that easy to define respect, partly because people have different ideas about what constitutes respectful and disrespectful behavior. For example, one person might feel strongly that being yelled at is a serious sign of disrespect. Meanwhile, that person's partner may have grown up in a home where yelling at each other was considered proof you were involved in the conversation.

Nevertheless, almost everybody agrees that certain behaviors definitely show respect. People feel respected when others:

- Pay attention to them when they are speaking, without interrupting

- Listen carefully to what they say and then respond thoughtfully to their ideas

- Speak politely without swearing at them

- Think ahead about what to say and do to avoid offending them

- Regularly attend to their wants and needs

Unfortunately, people sometimes believe that their partners fail to respect them. They complain that their partners interrupt them when they speak. They say they feel almost invisible because what they think, feel, want, and need don't seem to matter. Sadly, they report that over time this problem has worsened: "She used to listen when I spoke. Now she barely nods, and I know it's going in one ear and out the other." Indeed, people often seek counseling because they don't feel respected by their partners.

Sometimes the offender doesn't realize he or she is acting disrespectfully. That's partly because a lot of disrespectful behavior is more a matter of omission than commission. In other words, someone feels disrespected by his or her partner over a forgotten birthday, unexpected lateness for supper, distraction in the middle of a conversation, and so on. Still, damage occurs with every disrespectful act, whether conscious or unconscious, passive or active, deliberate or unintentional. These disrespectful behaviors eat away at the relationship like slow-acting acid, gradually dissolving the emotional glue that holds two people together.

These disrespectful acts often produce loud shouts of protest: "Turn off the TV and listen!" "You didn't hear what I just said, did you? Why don't you ever pay attention?" "I demand some respect around here!" Things generally go back to normal when the offender gets the message and changes his or her behavior. But sometimes nothing happens; the protests are ineffective, falling on the same deaf ears that prompted the complaint. And that's when the disrespected party is tempted to get the need for respect met elsewhere. Later, when the committed partner challenges his or her actions, the straying partner might attack angrily: "Well, if you treated me with half the respect that _____ does, I wouldn't need to spend time away from home."

Could your partner be justifying his or her emotional affair by claiming that you're disrespectful? Ask yourself these questions:

Does your partner frequently claim that you don't respect him or her?

Are there specific things your partner wants from you that would show respect?

Do you feel disrespected by your partner? (Often, disrespect goes two ways. If you feel disrespected, so might your partner.)

More of the Five A's: Attention, Appreciation, Acceptance, Admiration, and Affirmation

"My girlfriend ignores me."

"Nobody in my family appreciates me."

"My husband doesn't accept me for who I am."

"I'd sure like to get a compliment once in a while."

"I get the feeling that my wife tolerates me, at best. My friend helps me feel good about myself."

Human beings are interactive by nature. We need for others, especially our committed partners, to notice us. That cup of coffee in the morning, the gentle "welcome home" hug after work, and a "good night" before turning off the lights confirm that you and your partner are important to each other. Just receiving those small acknowledgments helps us feel connected to the universe. Take them away, and most people feel lonely and deprived. That may be when they start thinking about finding someone else with whom they could feel this bond.

A couple with a healthy, thriving relationship regularly confirms their mutual importance in five different but overlapping ways. We have labeled these methods the five *a*'s: attention, appreciation, acceptance, admiration, and affirmation.

Of the five, attention is the simplest, but perhaps most critical, connector. To attend means we look at, listen to, and literally touch our partners. The core message is "I choose to take time to notice you." It feels great to be noticed this way. People feel empty when they go unnoticed. They often complain about being taken for granted.

Getting attention from one's committed partner is the meat and potatoes of a relationship. Dessert comes next, in the form of receiving appreciation. The message of appreciation is "I like what you do." Maybe it's the way you fold laundry, smile, or write your blog. It feels wonderful to get a compliment, more so when it comes from your partner, the one person in the world you most hope to please. People swell with pride (in a good way) when complimented. However, they shrink into themselves when they go unrewarded.

Acceptance is the third member of the *a* family. Here, the message is "It's okay with me for you to be you. I like you the way you are." That means you don't have to change to be acceptable. Isn't this one of the best reasons to be in a committed relationship? It's such a relief to feel that you can be yourself with someone. You don't have to wear a mask. You don't have to apologize because you're not your partner's mother, father, or ex-lover. You can let down your hair and relax.

The fourth *a* stands for admiration. Now the message becomes "I can learn from you"—the way you think, how you organize the budget, your gracefulness with company, your thoughtfulness. We value the people we admire. When we admire our committed partners, we realize that we can become better by letting ourselves learn from them.

The last *a* is for affirmation, which is the most spiritually connecting of the five. Now the underlying message is "I celebrate your existence." The affirming partner feels wonderful that his or her partner lives on this planet, amazed and humbled in the partner's presence. We have a sense of awe that someone this special could be a part of our lives.

The five *a*'s are a beautiful part of a healthy relationship. Unfortunately, sometimes one partner goes looking for them outside the committed partnership. To determine whether that could be your situation, ask yourself these questions:

Does your partner complain about not receiving any of the five *a*'s?

Which of the five *a*'s would be most important for your partner to receive?

Have giving and receiving these gifts been a regular part of your relationship?

To Feel More Important and Special

"The kids, her sisters, the dog—they're all more important to her than I."

"I asked myself when the last time was that he made me feel really special, and I couldn't remember."

"My friend helps me feel unique and important, that I truly matter."

It's all about priorities. Most people want to believe that their partners view them as the top priority in their lives. Okay, maybe the kids are just as important, but that's it. Other than that, each individual hopes to see that marvelous look in his or her partner's eyes, the one that says, "Of all the people in the world I could've chosen, I picked you and I'm sure glad I did." That look, often accompanied by a warm smile and maybe a hug, helps people feel absolutely safe and secure in their relationships.

Happily committed partners tend to overrate their mates. They often rank them perhaps 10 percent smarter, smoother, stronger, and sexier than they actually are. But that's good; it means they value their partners a lot. They see their partners as special. Furthermore, they defend their partners against anyone who'd insult or disrespect them. They insist that the rest of the world honor and respect their partners.

But what happens when someone quits sensing that warm glow of appreciation and feels disappointed, cheated, lonely, and discouraged? Perhaps this person starts holding back as well, so that now neither partner ends up feeling special and important. The best thing that could happen would be for this couple to make every effort to rekindle their love and respect for each other. Each of them needs to remember that the other individual is indeed a wonderful human being. The result can be that the relationship not only is salvaged but also becomes richer and more intimate. On the other hand, one or both partners might begin an emotional affair in the hope of regaining the feeling of being really special to another.

How important is it to you to feel special like this?

How important is it to your partner?

Do you think your partner may be looking to another for that special feeling?

More Loving Friendship (Agape)

"My husband and I used to be best friends. I trusted him with everything. But that was long ago."

"I want to feel loved again. Not sexual love though, the kind of love one very good friend has for another."

"I think the Greek or Latin word for what I want is 'agape,' you know, a wonderful caring for each other that has nothing to do with physical attraction."

There's sometimes a fine line between erotic attraction and emotional intimacy. Nevertheless, many people having emotional affairs absolutely insist that they are not interested in becoming sexually involved with their emotional-affair partners. They often claim they simply aren't physically attracted to them. If they admit some physical interest, they state strongly that they would never act on the attraction because it would ruin the special friendship. They're usually right about that too. Once an emotional affair becomes a total affair, the relationship changes drastically. Emotional connection then frequently becomes subordinated to sexual matters. And if such a pair's sex life begins to go badly, the entire relationship is usually destroyed.

We could coin a new term for the hoped for result of an emotional affair: loving friendship. However, we don't really need to do so, because the ancient Greeks already created a word for this special form of nonsexual love. They called it *agape* ("ah-GAHP-eh"). A dictionary definition of agape is "unselfish love of one person for another without sexual implications; brotherly love" (Random House Unabridged 1993, s.v. "Agape").

Couples in American society usually want a lot from each other. It's not enough just to share the burdens of making an income and raising kids. They also seek a mutually satisfying sexual partnership. And, on top of all that, they often expect to be each other's best friend. In some ways the best-friend idea is the American version of agape. We put so much energy into the nuclear family that there's little time to develop deeply meaningful friendships with others. Instead, we want our relationship partners to also be our closest confidants.

A pair of familiar complaints frequently reflects this desire for an agape-like friendship within the context of a sexual relationship: "Can't you ever give me a hug without it turning sexual?" and "Why don't you ever want to sit and talk anymore?"

It's tremendously rewarding to have an agape-like friendship within a committed relationship. However, partners who greatly desire agape but feel that it's missing from their committed relationships can feel cheated. They may seek someone outside the relationship to meet that need. Remember that what counts here is the straying individual's perception, not necessarily the actual situation. In other words, the person having the emotional affair might mistakenly deem the committed partner as disinterested in being his or her best friend. Mistaken or not, that person looks elsewhere for someone with whom he or she can find that special nonsexual friendship.

> Does your partner complain that you aren't a good enough friend?
>
> Can you think of times when the two of you really sat down and talked the way good friends speak to each other?
>
> How important to each of you is the idea of being each other's best friend?

We've suggested many reasons why your partner might be having an emotional affair. He or she may want more emotional connection or understanding; more praise and less criticism; more freedom, action, emotional intensity, or respect; more of the five *a*'s: attention, appreciation, acceptance, admiration, and affirmation; to feel more important and special; or to have more loving friendship (*agape*). The exercise that follows will help you decide which of these reasons might best fit your situation, based on your understanding of your partner's basic wants and needs.

Dealing with the "I Wants"

Goal: Assess How "I Want..." Affects You and Your Partner

We have discussed a number of "I want..." areas that are significant to most relationships. Now it's time for you (or you and your partner) to consider how the "I wants" affect your relationship. Following is a list of areas addressed in this chapter, part of a table for you to rate (as well as you can) what your partner wanted from you at the start of your relationship, what you wanted from your partner at the start, and how your own and your partner's desires have changed over time.

Remember, you're estimating or guessing from your perspective. The rankings you put for your partner are your guesses. Here's the code to help you rank the items on this table: use a scale from 1 to 10, with 1 meaning that this want was desired hardly at all, and 10 meaning that it was extremely important to one or both of you.

When you get to the last two columns, just use an up arrow (↑) or down arrow (↓) to indicate whether you now want more or less of this quality, and what your partner wants now. All relationships change, and partners don't always change in the same direction or at the same time. In the last row of the table, where it says "Other," write in a quality that's important in your relationship that we didn't mention here.

Wants	Partner	Self	Partner's Change	My Change
Emotional Connection				
Understanding				
More Praise				
Less Criticism				
Freedom				
Action				
Emotional Intensity				
Respect				
Other				

Now, review your table. How did you start in your partnership? Have you changed? How about your partner (as far as you can tell)? What directions are you two going in now? Think about how you might begin to talk to your partner about these changes you see.

Goal: Add More Praise and Less Criticism to Your Relationship

Few people really enjoy criticism, especially repeated, angry, or name-calling criticism. Some of us don't want to think we do things wrong, some of us are embarrassed when we don't do something right, and often enough our partners will find something to criticize just when we've done something we consider good. On the other hand, many of us have grown up learning how to criticize better than to praise, or do so to control our environments because we assume that our own way is the best.

Praise, when it's honest, is something most of us like. If we're not very used to getting praise, we can learn to take it in and enjoy it. And when we get used to it—why, we just want more. The truth is that praise is more powerful than criticism just for that reason. Praise includes three of the five *a*'s, reassures us, and improves our self-esteem too. Generally, in any relationship, what you give the most attention is often what you get; so do you really want to give so much attention to how you and others do things wrong? When someone praises something you do, you feel good and want to do something for that person in the future.

One warning: It's easy to turn praise into criticism. For example, imagine watching your partner vacuum the floor. "Thanks for vacuuming, but you missed a spot" is really not praise. When you put the "but" in the sentence, you take the good stuff back. So make sure to keep your praise separate from criticism. Also remember that your partner probably vacuums (and washes dishes, cooks, and so on) a little differently than you do. Different, though, doesn't mean worse. There are lots of equally good ways to vacuum, wash dishes, or cook.

- Find and list five ways you can praise your partner.

- Find and list five ways you can praise yourself.

- For a day (or a week), use praise and don't be hard on either yourself or your partner.

Goal: Remember the Five *A*'s—Attention, Appreciation, Acceptance, Admiration, and Affirmation

Write down this prayer, which is modeled on the traditional Serenity Prayer but incorporates the five *a*'s. Read it once in the morning and once in the evening, and put a copy under your pillow for a week.

Let the "God" in this prayer be spirit or higher power as you best understand it.

> *"God, grant me the ability to pay attention to the important things in my life, to appreciate what I do and what my partner does, to accept that we are different and that there really isn't anybody who's easy to live with, to admire the way my partner does things, even if I might do them differently, and to affirm both myself and my partner as we figure out the problems and issues of growing."*

4

Whose Fault Is It? Your Partner's? Your Rival's? Yours?

It would be difficult to write a book about emotional affairs without dealing with blame, guilt, and responsibility. But who should take responsibility for this unfortunate occurrence? Is blame to be placed solely upon the partner who strayed? How much responsibility must the third party take? And how about you, the aggrieved partner? Is it fair to hold you blameless, a totally innocent victim? Or do you need to examine the ways you may have contributed to your partner's looking to someone else for an emotional alliance?

We'll begin with three relatively simple ways to handle the situation. Specifically, we'll consider placing all the blame on your straying partner, your rival (the third party), or you. Then we'll even consider trying to exclude the whole issue of blame and guilt. And finally we'll suggest a better way to think about blame in an emotional affair. Our goal will be to help you consider the "us" component of your relationship and how problems there might have made your partner's emotional affair more likely.

IT'S ALL YOUR PARTNER'S FAULT!

It's tempting to cast all the responsibility on the straying partner. That would mean it's entirely his or her fault. Then we could treat you, the non-straying partner, as an entirely blameless victim. This approach would be consistent with the way female victims of domestic abuse are told, appropriately, that nothing they do merits their partners' use of violence against them.

You can probably see the problems with taking this path. First, holding one person entirely responsible for a mutual problem is simplistic. That process may be necessary in a life-threatening situation in which the victim's feelings of guilt over her alleged failures might keep her from protecting herself. However, nobody's life is threatened during an emotional affair. There may be nasty arguments, but there's no physical brutality. (If there is, we advise you to get help with that serious problem before even attempting to tackle this one.)

Equally important, an explanation that puts all the responsibility on your partner leaves you with few viable options. About all you can do is leave the strayer or demand that he or she stop the emotional affair. That means that only your partner has the power to change things.

A quick note here though: we definitely expect the straying partner to take a very honest and self-critical look at his or her behavior. We'll say more about that later in this chapter.

IT'S ALL YOUR FAULT!

Another overly simple possibility would be to side with the straying partner, the one who's having the emotional affair. The strayer might claim that the only reason she got involved with someone else was because you treat her so badly. She'd then share a long list of all the things you do wrong, acts of commission and omission, that have driven her away. Now, instead of your having too little power, everything would supposedly be up to you. If you'd only mend your ways, maybe she'd bring her emotions back home. But you'd really be powerless once again, because your highly critical partner would act as judge and jury. And she'd probably look harder for things to criticize than for evidence of anything good, just to maintain the emotional affair. We call this one-sided view the "Tell it to the bartender" approach. This is a blaming model that doesn't increase understanding.

Still, it's important that you carefully evaluate anything you've said or done that might have played a part in your partner's emotional affair. We'll suggest a way for you to do that shortly.

IT'S ALL YOUR RIVAL'S FAULT

There's still one more candidate to blame for this terrible situation: the third party. Perhaps this person deliberately set out to steal your partner's attention. If only your rival had stayed away from your partner, the emotional affair would never had occurred. Instead, he made a concerted effort to become your partner's emotional confidant. He's become the person your partner turns to now, not you. Because of him, you've lost your best friend.

People who take this view tend to see their partners as somewhat naive and gullible. They reserve their anger, scorn, moral indignation, and even hatred for the rival. Their mission then becomes pulling their relatively innocent partners out of the emotional clutches of the intruder.

Now there may be some truth in these allegations. Third parties in emotional affairs can be intrusive. They can demand loyalty. Consciously or not, they can exert pressure upon one's partner to share feelings only with them. However, the problem with this approach is pretty obvious. Buying into this explanation diverts your attention away from your relationship with your partner at exactly the time you most need to concentrate on it. You'll waste a lot of time attacking your rival instead of dealing with your mutual issues. Besides, your partner needs to take responsibility for his or her actions. Giving all that responsibility to the third person mistakenly takes your partner off the hook. Enabling your straying partner won't help matters.

There may come a time when that rival must be confronted. But the person doing the confronting should be your partner, not you. For now, you'd be much better off to put your rival on the back burner so you can stay focused on your relationship issues.

Real relationship problems are complicated and confusing. That's why these crude models don't help much. It's not just your partner, it's not just you, and it's not just your rival. Instead, we need a better way of viewing what occurs during an emotional affair. Ultimately we want an approach that maximizes your power to affect the situation.

IT'S NOBODY'S FAULT

A fourth possibility would be to skirt around the whole issue of blame. We could treat this emotional affair as an unfortunate circumstance that really isn't anybody's fault. Sometimes bad things just happen in marriages. Why does it have to be a matter of casting blame? Doesn't casting blame just make people feel awful or get defensive?

This approach could be helpful in situations where the straying partner more or less drifted into an emotional affair and would really like to end it quickly. By blaming no one, it's possible to pretend the emotional affair never happened. One risk here, though, is ignoring the actual issues that exist within the committed relationship. What will keep those same concerns from arising again? What will happen if those same unresolved problems lead your partner into another emotional affair?

A second point is that people heal best after an emotional affair ends when everyone owns up to his or her shortcomings and wrongdoings. This is important because meaningful promises have been broken; morally significant commitments have been violated. The result of this "cast no blame" model could be that no one offers any apologies or attempts to make amends. That could in turn mean that one or both partners are left with smoldering resentments.

There is such a thing as good guilt. It's the guilt that leads to heartfelt confession. Good guilt also spurs people to change their thoughts, feelings, and actions. Hopefully, in this situation each person's willingness to accept personal responsibility will also lead to the end of the emotional affair and the beginning of a stronger, healthier committed relationship.

IT'S ME, YOU, AND US

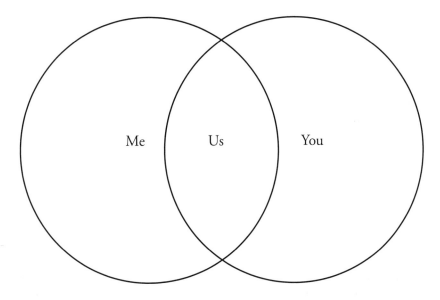

Me   Us   You

Here's a useful approach. Notice the two intersecting hoops in the figure. The right side of one hoop is labeled "YOU." That part is about the partner engaged in the emotional affair. What has your partner done or failed to do that led up to the emotional affair? We're not talking about your partner's relationship with you (that comes next). Instead, we want you to make a list of your partner's individual behaviors and personality traits that have contributed to his or her straying away. For example, your partner may have a serious drinking problem he's not willing to face. Perhaps he's quite pessimistic by nature and so only focuses on the bad things that happen in life. Maybe he hates the very idea of making a long-term emotional commitment to anyone.

You probably realize that you cannot single-handedly change your partner's behavior or personality. But you can challenge your partner to take a good look at these negative characteristics. You can insist that any real reconciliation between the two of you include your partner's commitment to work on these character flaws. And you have the right to choose to leave the relationship if you become convinced that your partner cannot or will not change.

Hopefully, at some point soon, your straying partner will want to think through what she has done and what she could do differently. If and when this happens she'll need to make a careful, thorough, and honest moral survey of her behavior since even before the emotional affair began. This will involve a definite amount of soul searching and will necessitate letting go of the "It's your fault; you made me do this" argument with which she has justified her behavior. (Note: readers who are engaged in an emotional affair can begin that moral inventory by reading chapter 6 of this book.)

Now please turn your attention to the left edge of the hoop. That "ME" area is the place for you to think about how you may have helped contribute to the problems in your relationship. Now remember, nobody's saying it's entirely your fault. It's not that at all. However, it can only help if you're willing to take an honest and thorough look at whatever you may have done or are still doing to create emotional distance between you and your partner. But remember as you approach this task that your main goal is to be honest with yourself. That means different things to different people. Specifically, if you're a self-blamer, guard against taking on too much guilt for your partner's behavior. On the other hand, if you tend to blame others, open yourself up to some painful self-criticism. Try to strike a balance between "It's all my fault" and "I've done nothing wrong at all"; don't be either a villain or a victim. The goal is to have you take a serious look at how your actions might be contributing to your partner's behavior. However, the last thing we want to do is lay a huge guilt trip on you. The question is this: how can you best take responsibility for what you do so that you can change your actions without taking on your partner's guilt?

The "Us" Component

The area in the figure where the hoops intersect is labeled "US." That middle area represents the ways the two of you have interacted that inadvertently helped produce the emotional affair. This is the place to notice the communication problems you run into regularly. For instance, the two of you might participate in endless repetitive fights. These are battles that get repeated continually, almost as if they were played out on a film loop.

The "us" area is pregnant with positive possibility. It's an area that you can affect individually (for instance, by declining to keep arguing during a repetitive disagreement). But it's also a place for the two of you to work on together as you try to reconcile. Hopefully, if not now then sometime soon, both you and your partner will look closely at how you disconnected from each other. Then you can start to reconnect. (We will help you explore the "us" area of mutual reconciliation in chapter 7.)

This "us" area is vital because every partnership takes on a life of its own. The ways any two people interact develop into predictable routines after a few months. Some of these patterns are healthy, providing both partners with a sense of connection. For example, quiet Sunday mornings reading the paper together, mutually understood glances on the way to the bedroom, playful pretend fights, and so on help strengthen a relationship. But what we'll discuss next are several unfortunate patterns that couples may develop over time. These patterns decrease one or both partners' emotional satisfaction. They increase the likelihood that someone will emotionally stray from the partnership.

We're not trying to make excuses for your straying partner. That individual still must take responsibility for his or her actions. Indeed, the choice your partner has made to have an emotional affair obviously damages your mutual relationship. Still, it's important for you to think about your relationship as an interactive system. In other words, everything you do affects your partner and everything your partner does affects you. Right now it's likely that your mutual system is like a car with a bad muffler. Yes, it's still running, but it's in need of a few repairs. The difference is in the kind of repairs needed. Yours are emotional, not mechanical.

Following are seven negative emotional patterns that cause problems between partners in committed relationships.

MUTUAL ANGER AND HOSTILITY

"We just keep fighting, fighting, fighting. Then we avoid each other for a couple of days. Then we try to reconnect, but it only leads to more arguments."

Anger is a valuable emotion. This strong feeling serves to inform partners that something is wrong and needs immediate attention. But anger is like a very strong chili pepper. A little goes a long way and a lot makes things too hot to handle. Over time, when a couple experiences too much anger too frequently, anger becomes a distance-creating emotion, pushing partners away from each other. This is particularly true when the two partners habitually argue and complain. That's when virtually every conversation starts badly and ends worse. Eventually one or both partners develop a chronically hostile attitude toward the other. Now, instead of seeing your partner as a friend and ally, you start to see that person as an opponent or enemy.

The partners in angry relationships often show anger in different ways. One person may grumble and mutter in a barely audible voice. Another may shout and scream in total frustration. A third individual might become passive-aggressive, demonstrating anger mostly by forgetting, stalling, and generally failing to be responsible. A fourth is a master of the cold shoulder, refusing to talk about issues while freezing his or her partner with an "if looks could kill" stare. Whichever method angry partners use to express themselves, though, will be used frequently. Almost inevitably, the responding partner will react with anger as well. Quite probably, as in a highly competitive poker game, the responding partner will not only match the other's anger but raise the stakes by adding new insults or accusations.

Chronic anger doesn't force anyone into an emotional affair. But who looks forward enthusiastically to coming home for yet another fight? And what if one of these battling people befriends someone with whom he or she never argues? The very anger that drives two people apart might also push them toward others.

LACK OF EMOTIONAL COMMITMENT

"Neither of us really jumped into this marriage with both feet. It's as if we've each kept our emotional bags packed all these years."

The partners in some relationships seem tremendously cautious about making true emotional commitments to each other. Instead, they keep a safe distance from each other, seldom sharing their deeper feelings. They may get along decently, but there's an unstated rule prohibiting emotional intimacy. These couples function more like business partners than best friends. They raise the kids, build their home, save for retirement, and go on vacations together just fine. They just don't dig very deep emotionally.

People in these relationships often grew up in homes that de-emphasized the world of feelings. Their parents would've been generally inexpressive, seldom hugging or showing affection, and they would've discussed any serious issues privately. Their children would've received little encouragement or training about emotional intimacy. A predictable result is that these children would be attracted to relatively nonemotional or unexpressive potential partners.

You may be asking yourself why these partners would ever get into an emotional affair when they appear disinterested in emotional intimacy. The answer is that sometimes people change. Perhaps they develop a vague sense that they're missing something important. Then they observe other couples sharing emotional intimacies and apparently feeling good about it. They want that mysterious something too. Now they certainly could approach their partners on the theory that maybe they also desire a deeper, more emotional relationship. They could do that. But they don't, because they've built up years of rules and habits against that kind of sharing. Their inertia pushes them to continue in their old, familiar, but now unsatisfying, routines. Meanwhile, they go looking for someone new with whom they can meet their newfound yearning for emotional closeness.

MUTUAL DISTRUST

"He says I betrayed him by talking with my family about our problems. But he broke my trust years ago after he laughed at me when I cried."

Love is often said to form the strongest bond between people. However, trust is equally powerful. Trust is the glue that tells partners they can rely on each other. Without trust, relationships become shallow as each partner keeps a watchful eye on the other. Certainly any relationship devoid of trust seldom lasts very long.

Trust builds, or fails to build, in many different areas, such as financial accountability, sexual fidelity, and long-term planning. But the most important sphere to discuss here is emotional trust. Emotional trust grows whenever either partner shares his or her emotions with the other and in turn receives a positive response. It's not only that Betty chooses to tell Jake how sad she feels that her beloved cat is sick. Jake must also respond thoughtfully, with caring rather than dismissiveness or criticism.

> Caring response: "Yes, I feel bad for you. I know how much she means to you."

> Dismissive response: "Oh, will you please just get over it? She's just a cat."

> Critical response: "You're stupid to care that much for a cat. You're really a nut case."

Sharing emotions makes people vulnerable. That means the emotion receiver must honor the speaker's need for privacy. One sure way to destroy trust is for the receiver to tell other people things the speaker thought would be kept private.

Yet another way to lessen emotional trust occurs when someone tells emotional lies to his or her partner. A good example would be for Jake to tell Betty that he feels good about her working late when, in actuality, he has become angry and resentful.

Ideally couples build trust over time. The relationship itself can then be said to be trustworthy. However, it's all too possible for trust to be replaced with mutual distrust. This happens when both parties decide they really cannot safely share their true emotions with their partners. When asked why, they may cite a specific occasion when they felt betrayed. But single incidents can usually be forgiven. What's worse is when both people feel their partners have repeatedly responded badly to their emotional disclosures. That's when they may start searching for someone they can better trust with their emotions.

EMOTIONAL OVERDEPENDENCE

"Sometimes it feels as if we're so close that it's suffocating. We have no separate identities. It's not good when two people need each other more than they want each other."

Family therapists use the term *symbiotic* to describe the specific type of problematic relationship in which the two partners become very tightly bound together. They become mutually dependent to the point where both people give up much of their individual identities. Instead, they live in a world of "us" and "we." They often have no separate friendships because all their energy goes into shared connections. They frequently work together as well. They've essentially thrown all their eggs in one basket. They cling tightly to each other because they view life as if it's they against the world.

There's no question here about emotional connection. Symbiotically bound pairs can spend hours each day sharing every morsel of emotion they feel. Indeed, one rule is that nothing should be held back. Little distinction is made between privacy and secrecy. If one partner were to withhold any feelings, the other would feel hurt, even betrayed.

Symbiotic relationships suffer from one major problem, namely, that such partners have difficulty maintaining any breathing room. Eventually one or both partners may experience a hidden longing to get away. Most often the complaint will take the form of suggesting doing some activities apart. But sometimes what that translates into is that one partner wants to spend time with somebody else. Since these individuals are used to intense emotional relationships, they can quickly become caught up in emotional affairs with third parties. The original partner then feels tremendously lonely and is stunned that the very person who recently shared virtually everything with him or her now has become totally emotionally embroiled with another.

CONTINUING POWER BATTLES

"We're two stubborn people. Neither of us will give in. We seem to disagree about everything."

Many couples battle continuously over who has power and control within the relationship. These pairs seem to make it a point of honor to disagree with each other about every decision, no matter how major or minor. Should their bathroom be painted or papered? Should their kids go to public or private schools? Should they get a divorce or stay together? You can bet they'll disagree about each and every one of these choices because that's what they do.

The battle here, of course, isn't about bathrooms or schools or divorce. It's really all about power and control. Whoever wins any argument gains the upper hand for a little while. But neither partner can accept losing. Soon there will be another disagreement and another and another. Or perhaps this couple will simply recycle the same argument. We call these disagreements "Here we go again" fights because they've been going on for so long that both sides have their lines perfectly memorized.

It's not even that these partners are angry with each other. True, their anger might flare up in the middle of a disagreement. But anger is just another tool in the toolbox that might help them get their way. Besides, they continue to dispute every issue, even when they're happy with each other.

These interminable battles over power and control are emotionally expensive. They drain each person's energy. They destroy hope and optimism. They turn partners into opponents in an endless game of "king of the hill." Eventually, to avoid yet another argument, the individuals involved quit even bringing up things. Important decisions are left unmade and are never even discussed.

A partner stuck in power and control battles may long to meet someone with whom he or she doesn't constantly disagree. That's when the partner becomes vulnerable to going outside the committed relationship. The dissatisfied partner finds a third person with whom to develop an emotional affair and then ends up arguing forever about that issue with the committed partner along with everything else.

OVERFOCUS ON FAMILY OR CHILDREN

"We do wonderfully with the children. But that's our only common bond. They're about all we ever talk about."

If you saw Terry and Louisa at the park with their children, you'd think they were a perfectly content couple. They're always smiling and laughing. They take turns giving the kids pushes on the swings. The picnic dinner smells absolutely delicious. They'll even talk your ear off about the children. They are one happy family.

But that's it. That's all they are. Terry and Louisa are part of a family, but they're not really a couple. The sad fact is that they have nothing to talk about except their children. They share no common interests. They have no long-term goals. They can't imagine their life together after the kids grow up. They'll probably simply inhabit the same house.

This couple lives in an emotional desert. Rather, they reside on an oasis in that desert as long as they focus on their children. Within that sanctuary they can be happy, sad, scared, and so on. They can and do share many feelings. But take away the kids and that oasis vanishes as if it were a mirage. They don't share feelings as a couple in that desert because they don't have any to share.

Terry and Louisa aren't exactly lonely. After all, their children certainly keep them occupied. But they do have a nagging sense that life would be better if they could share more than their children. They'd like to have someone with whom they could really connect emotionally. And once again, one or both parties might be tempted to look to someone outside their committed relationship to meet that unfulfilled desire.

OVERSENSITIVITY TO INSULT

"We're very sensitive people whose feelings get hurt easily. We end up being defensive around each other. Lately our favorite phrase has become 'What do you mean by that?'"

Emotional sensitivity is by and large a positive trait. The person who regularly notices how another's words and actions affect him or her emotionally gains important information about how to respond. For instance, a woman on a first date might feel a little sad when her date talks about the recent death of his pet retriever. That feeling of sadness creates an emotional bridge between them. On the other hand she might feel angry and back away if he makes a thoughtlessly chauvinistic remark.

The most important person to tune in to emotionally is your partner. That's the person whose words and deeds have the most power to hurt or heal you. When a relationship goes well, partners come to expect mostly positive messages from each other, messages that will trigger good feelings. However, nobody's perfect. Even in the best relationships, both partners inevitably say and do things that make the other feel bad. Each occasion is painful and hard to forget. Over time such incidents can build up in both people's minds, especially if the couple isn't very adept at repairing the damage they do to each other. Finally, these individuals begin to expect to be attacked emotionally by their partners. Now they become focused on the pain to the point where they may completely ignore each other's positive communications. Such couples have now become mutually oversensitive to emotional attack.

Some couples become remarkably thin skinned as their relationship develops. By that, we mean that they both listen carefully for any critical sign in their partners' words and actions. And, as you might suspect, people who expect criticism invariably find it. They react as if they've been slapped in the face. "You're being mean to me," they claim. "You said that just to hurt my feelings."

Meanwhile, accused partners frequently take an innocent stance: "I don't know what you're talking about. I didn't mean to hurt you.

I don't even know what I said that bothers you so much." Then they add the clincher: "You're just being too sensitive!" That's when things get really messy. Now the accusing partner feels doubly attacked, first by whatever was said and then by this nasty putdown. At the same time the responding partner gets more and more defensive in denying that any injury was intended.

This kind of selective oversensitivity can be a one-way street, with only one person playing out the role of the highly sensitive, easily hurt partner while the other partner gets more and more defensive. But sometimes both parties play both roles, alternating between accuser and accused. The end result is that each person believes the other is inattentive to good things and too easily hurt by bad interactions.

Again, the groundwork has been laid for one or both partners to begin an emotional affair. This time, strayers search for someone who is "nice" to them as opposed to "mean." They'll be attracted to third parties who give them praise and make them feel good about themselves. They'll also appreciate those who seem to fully understand their emotional pain without telling them to grow a tougher hide.

HEALING AND HOPE

You will break important ground by carefully examining the "us" part of your relationship. Doing so will help you see how your mutual interactions could become more rewarding for both of you.

We strongly believe that an emotional affair does not have to signal the inevitable death of a committed relationship. Instead, it's possible for a couple to heal their wounds, provided, of course, that the straying partner ends the emotional affair and recommits to the original relationship. Healing will happen most quickly and deeply when both partners take a long look at what they've done wrong and what they could do right. Then, as each partner accepts personal responsibility, together they can explore the "us" component of their relationship. Together they can improve and enrich their partnership. What better way could there be to lessen the likelihood that either person will develop another emotional affair?

Rank the Seven Common Problems Couples Encounter

We've identified seven common problems that couples encounter. Some of them may be quite important to you, others less so. Please rank them from 1 to 7, with 1 representing the problem you feel most negatively affects your relationship, and 7 representing the least problematic issue.

_____ Mutual anger and hostility

_____ Lack of emotional commitment

_____ Mutual distrust

_____ Emotional overdependence

_____ Continuing power battles

_____ Overfocus on family or children

_____ Oversensitivity to insult

Do you think your partner would rank these problems in the same way?

Later, when we talk about healing your relationship in chapter 7, you'll begin that process by addressing the worst (highest ranked) problems first.

A Closer Look at the Seven Negative Emotional Patterns

Mutual Anger and Hostility

We do a lot of marriage counseling in our clinic in Eau Claire, Wisconsin. It's painful to watch the way some couples attack each other mercilessly when they first come in. A person can be just plain mean-spirited toward the supposed love of his or her life. Blaming, shaming, guilt-tripping, name calling, swearing, screaming, and so on—you name it, and couples are doing it. What's worse is that such behavior becomes automatic and habitual. No matter what one partner says, the other attacks: "That's stupid! You're wrong. It's not that way. That never happened." They wouldn't consider giving each other the benefit of the doubt. They wouldn't dream of saying anything nice. Essentially such couples have declared war on one another.

How much does your relationship sound like this? If so, your mutual hostility and anger are getting in the way of having a good partnership, raising your defenses high against each other and pushing you apart.

Here's one thing you can do to change this nasty pattern. You can decide that your partner is your friend, not your enemy. Then ask yourself how friends treat friends, and act accordingly.

Lack of Emotional Commitment

Some couples have difficulty sharing feelings and ideas, sadness and excitement with each other. But taking the risk of sharing feelings and letting your partner know who you are injects a thing called "vitality" into a relationship. So do loving glances, small touches, and understanding for your partner's feelings.

Lack of emotional commitment means that the two of you haven't decided yet that sharing your feelings should be a vital part of your relationship. However, a commitment to sharing emotions needs to be added since at least one of you has gone elsewhere for that purpose. Notice that we're not just talking about the skill of sharing feelings. Almost anybody can learn these skills (such as empathy) with practice. We're talking about making a deep, mutual commitment to valuing emotional connection with your partner.

Nobody can force another person to make this kind of commitment. But eventually, making a mutual commitment to emotional sharing will be critical to healing your relationship. The earlier you can begin discussing this possibility together, the better will be your chances of getting past the emotional affair.

Mutual Distrust

An example of mutual distrust is a couple who repeatedly bring up past betrayals—from two, four, or thirty years ago—with incidents to prove their partners cannot be trusted. Both partners do this, but each blames the other. They've gotten used to giving each other negative feedback. Lies about money, sexuality (such as, "I'm on birth control"), fidelity, and drinking or drugs can all lead to mutual distrust. Mutual distrust leads to the mutual hostility mentioned previously, as well as the temptation to check on the other partner, reading his or her mail or personal journal, and so forth.

To heal mutual distrust, each partner needs to make and keep a commitment to honesty. The idea is first to be honest yourself, and only then expect or insist upon honesty from your partner. Trust will slowly replace distrust when you both can be counted upon to tell the truth.

Emotional Overdependence

Usually emotional overdependence takes root when members of a couple feel insecure when alone and "complete" when together. This works for only a while though. When this happens, one or both partners have trouble with normal periods of separation. That difficulty sets the stage for friction, arguing, and jealous accusations. A better goal is interdependence, where partners can be together or apart and enjoy their time either way.

You are a complete person whether you know it or not, and so is your partner. Have you been leaning on each other too much?

Here's something you can do individually if you identify with being overdependent: make a list of your strengths. You have them, and you need to find them. Some characteristics can be either strengths or weaknesses, such as being stubborn. List those characteristics as well. When you have listed as many as you can think of, ask family and friends for the ways they see you as strong.

Continuing Power Battles

The more you and your partner fight for control, the more difficult it is for you to relax, enjoy each other's company, and share vulnerabilities. That makes it important for the two of you to reduce battling over power and control whenever you can.

What are five issues in daily life that you and your partner battle over? Are you the pushy one, or do you dig in your heels and refuse to move? Do you play both parts?

Here's something for you to consider if you want to quit battling so much over power and control. What one area would you be willing to cede control over to your partner, and what one area would you take full responsibility for if your partner agreed?

Overfocus on Family or Children

Have you and your partner been so busy raising your family that you've forgotten your relationship? Sometimes partners get so busy producing the perfect family, house, yard, social life, and so on that they forget to take time together. How true does this ring for your relationship?

This concern is easy to solve in theory. Just choose to frequently make time for each other. But habitual patterns are hard to break, so sometimes it's hard to put the obvious solution into practice. Nevertheless, as a couple you'll always be vulnerable to an emotional affair until you clearly choose each other as friends and companions. Don't let habits and family activities keep you from celebrating your life together as a couple.

Can you think of three activities you and your partner could do together, just the two of you? What have you told yourself that stopped you from doing those activities in the past? What can you tell yourself now to get past those negative thoughts?

Oversensitivity to Insult

Remember "The Princess and the Pea" story? That princess was so sensitive to pain that she could feel a single pea placed under a stack of mattresses. Now why would that kind of reaction be considered good? Anybody so physically oversensitive would probably be given a medical diagnosis like fibromyalgia today.

Some relationships have not one but two emotional equivalents of that princess. All either partner has to do is look at the other a little funny, say something careless, or show up a few minutes late, and the other partner starts complaining or crying, or feeling hurt or sad. The oversensitive partner interprets these mild acts of thoughtlessness as proof that the offending partner doesn't respect or love him or her. This is a no-win situation, since inevitably every human being is occasionally thoughtless toward his or her partner.

Is oversensitivity a significant concern in your relationship? If so, you two will need to develop a little thicker skin with each other. We suggest that each of you make a list of the situations that trigger your exaggerated protests. Then commit to avoid taking personally every little thing your partner does wrong. Save your ammunition for the big things, the real problems that have threatened your partnership, and let go of the rest.

5

Facing the Truth: Confronting Your Partner About the Emotional Affair

So far we've discussed what emotional affairs look like, why people get into them, and the whole matter of blame and responsibility. All that's very important, of course, but it only provides background for what comes next, namely, the need to confront your partner about his or her behavior. This moment of truth cannot be evaded unless you intend to let the emotional affair run its course while you try to pretend that everything's okay.

We've divided this chapter into three sections, the first of which is named "Preparation." The goal here is to help you become mentally and emotionally ready to challenge your partner. The second section is "Taking Action," the actual engagement with your partner (which may take place over several sessions). Finally comes "The Aftermath," which is when you take stock of what's happened and how you're doing.

PREPARATION

There's no easy way to confront your partner about an emotional affair. That's just reality. So you need to take the time and effort to prepare carefully for what could be a painful encounter. Here are the important steps we'll cover next:

1. Prepare yourself physically, mentally, emotionally, and spiritually.

2. Develop and use your support system.

3. Don't stop yourself from confronting your partner.

4. Get your facts straight and specific.

5. Consider all possible interpretations of the facts.

6. Prepare to deal with your partner's defensiveness.

7. Know what you want to stop and start.

8. Be willing to compromise, but know your bottom line.

9. Plan the details of your initial intervention.

The Preparation Phase

You've got a lot to do before actually engaging your partner in conversation about the emotional affair. Your intervention will only succeed when you're fully prepared both psychologically and factually. So take enough time to think carefully about what actions you'll eventually take and in what way. We suggest that you follow these guidelines.

PREPARE YOURSELF PHYSICALLY, MENTALLY, EMOTIONALLY, AND SPIRITUALLY

There are two ways you can prepare physically for the challenge ahead. First, begin or continue an exercise program that includes running or taking walks, working out at the gym, participating in recreational sports, and so on. Your body will appreciate these activities a lot. So will your brain, if only because exercise will help you obsess less about the problem.

Second, you can begin or renew your relaxation practices. These include formal relaxation training (such as progressive muscle relaxation, in which you first tighten your muscles group by group and then fully relax them), breathing exercises (such as slowly taking ten full breaths in which you focus only upon inhaling and exhaling), and other ways you've discovered that really help you relax. However, beware of relaxing by using alcohol, mood-altering chemicals, food, or behaviors such as gambling or shopping. True, they may give you some temporary relief from your worries, but they could easily come back to haunt you. You need to relax, not escape from reality.

Next comes mental preparation. One major problem here is obsessive thinking. Obsession occurs when you spend so much time worrying about your partner's behavior that you lose track of the rest of your life. It's almost impossible to discipline your mind not to obsess at all. But you can lessen obsession by consciously limiting the time you allow yourself to think about the issue to a specific time of day and for a specific amount of time. For example, you can allow yourself to obsess for thirty minutes between 2 and 2:30 P.M. if that's a good time for you. Then the rest of the day (and especially at night), you must gently but firmly remind yourself that you've done your allotted obsessing for the day.

Keeping your partner's behavior in perspective is another useful mental preparation. Yes, this is a serious concern. Yes, it could endanger your relationship. But nobody's dying. You've probably gone through worse crises in your life than this one. Besides, you have enough strength and resilience within you to survive this problem. Keeping the emotional affair in perspective will help you avoid panicking and then saying or doing something damaging.

Emotional preparation is critically important. Remembering these two statements will help: (1) notice each and every one of your emotions now; (2) keep your emotions under control when speaking to your partner.

You need to notice each and every one of your emotions as they come up. Why do you need to notice all your emotions? Because each of them has an important but distinct message to give you. For instance, your fear might be telling you that your relationship is in big trouble and you need to run away from the danger. That's an important message, all right. But if you only attend to fear, you might miss your sadness's message reminding you of how much you'd miss your partner if you did break up. And then there's your anger's message to fight, fight, fight for what you want. Don't forget your joy's message that you can still have fun with your partner. Meanwhile, there are other emotions, such as loneliness, shame, and guilt, all asking for your attention. You will be cheating yourself of valuable information if you choose to ignore any of your emotions.

Keep your emotions under control when speaking to your partner. Most people, probably including your partner, have trouble dealing with extreme expressions of emotion. They either get defensive and aggressive, or shut down completely in the face of someone who's raging with anger, shaking in fear, suicidally sad, or hysterically happy. So do your ventilating elsewhere if you need to—on your own, with a friend, or in counseling—but keep your emotions under control during your conversations, especially when you confront your partner about the emotional affair.

Spiritual preparation is your fourth challenge. Perhaps the most important thing you can do here is to focus on your partner's good soul. Try remembering your partner's positive qualities (which, after all, are the reasons you're in a relationship with him or her). Don't forget to link up with your own good soul as well, the part of you that has wonderful memories from the past, acceptance of the present, and hope for the future. This kind of positive soul-searching will help you approach the coming intervention with optimism and grace rather than with pessimism and cynicism.

You may want to seek spiritual guidance from a member of the religious community. Just be a little selective here. You'll need someone who understands the complexities of real-life relationships. We recommend you stay away from anyone, secular or religious, who approaches the subject of emotional affairs from an overly simplistic, absolutely good versus evil, perspective.

DEVELOP AND USE YOUR SUPPORT SYSTEM

You don't have to do this alone. Indeed, trying to solve this problem yourself would be a mistake. Without having people to bounce your ideas off of, you might miss some facts, distort the importance of other pieces of information, exaggerate your feelings, and end up acting foolishly.

Here are some criteria for deciding which people can help you the most. They should:

- Have earned your trust in previous difficult situations

- Be capable of challenging you when necessary if you're going off track

- Know enough about you and your relationship to be able to keep the facts straight

- Be able to stay calm in your storm

- Be good at helping you look at many different ways to take action rather than insisting you do only one thing

- Show caring for you while maintaining their boundaries so that you don't become dependent upon them

- Be able to understand your concerns and emotions, including your anger, while maintaining respect for your partner

- Have good common sense

Where do these people reside? Hopefully, you have a few friends and family members who meet these criteria. But also consider seeking help from counselors, clergy, people in self-help support groups, and those who've had to deal with emotional affairs themselves. Be careful with this last group though. Some individuals who've gone through emotional affairs stay way too angry and bitter for far too long. Look for "survivors" of these situations who've emerged hopeful and content.

DON'T STOP YOURSELF FROM CONFRONTING YOUR PARTNER

Conflict is not enjoyable. It can be downright scary. That's why most people prefer to avoid conflict whenever possible. But this is the time for courage. You'll need to overcome your fear of conflict to deal with this serious situation. It might help to remember that couples can and do recover from emotional affairs once they've been honestly addressed. The tricky part is figuring out how to challenge your partner so you can begin the healing process.

What about unnecessary guilt? Is useless guilt keeping you from challenging your partner? We're talking here about one specific kind of guilt. It's sometimes called "irrational" or "maladaptive" guilt. Irrational guilt occurs when you think you must've done something wrong that caused your partner's behavior, even though you're not to blame. Irrational guilt is a thief. It steals responsibility from others so you can have it all to yourself. You need to return that responsibility to its real owner, your partner, so that you can challenge him or her appropriately.

Maybe your idea of love keeps you quiet. You might believe that to confront your partner would be unloving. But what about not confronting him or her? How is it loving to ignore a real problem that has built a wall between the two of you? Won't it be more loving in the end if you can help your partner see how his or her behavior is damaging your relationship?

Perhaps you're a very forgiving person. That's definitely a strength—but not now. It's far too early to forgive your partner. Forgiveness is something to consider doing after your partner's negative behavior has ceased. Right now, you need acceptance more than forgiveness. You need to accept the truth that your relationship is in trouble and take definite action.

There may be other reasons, such as financial fears, that are hindering you right now. But we want to urge you to look for ways you can approach this problem before it gets worse.

GET YOUR FACTS STRAIGHT AND SPECIFIC

Marti's quite concerned about her partner Joe's interest in a woman named Samantha. She needs to confront him. The question is, what will she say?

How much impact do you think the following statement would have? "Joe, I kinda think something odd is going on between you and Samantha." Probably not much. Joe will likely respond with a remark such as, "Oh, there you go again, making something out of nothing." Now compare the initial, vague complaint with this statement: "Joe, five times last week, you spent over an hour on the phone with Samantha and then refused to tell me what you discussed." Obviously this second sentence is far more powerful than the first. Joe will have to answer his partner's documented complaint. That makes it much harder for him to turn the tables on her.

Just make sure you've got your facts straight. For instance, Marti will be accused of gross exaggeration of the problem if, in reality, Joe only spoke with Samantha for fifteen minutes a couple of times that week. Besides, you won't need to make anything up or exaggerate the problem if your partner really is having an emotional affair. You should be able to gather more than enough facts with a reasonable amount of detective work. Look for and write down activities that involve your partner's regularly making choices that take him or her away from you emotionally. Such choices would almost certainly include spending a lot of time visiting with, talking to, e-mailing, or text-messaging your rival. Your partner might refuse to discuss his or her activities with you. Your partner might mention frequently what a great friend so-and-so is or that they can discuss things together that he or she can't (and won't try) with you. Your partner might spend money purchasing gifts for this third party. So think about time, emotional energy, money, and evasiveness. Also, be able to contrast your partner's current behavior with past actions. One example would be reminding your partner that last year he or she attended almost every one of your son's basketball games, but has missed over half of them this year (have the missed dates at hand).

Perhaps now you're thinking that you don't want to spy on your partner. That's your choice, of course. Certainly stay within the boundaries of what you consider to be ethical behavior. However, don't expect anything good to happen unless you have clear, specific, and accurate information with which to confront your straying partner.

CONSIDER ALL POSSIBLE INTERPRETATIONS OF THE FACTS

Facts are meaningless without interpretations. And sometimes, when people are worried and anxious, they make the worst possible interpretations of their partners' behaviors. That's why it's important for you to consider different interpretations of your partner's actions.

Let's use the same example as in the previous section. Yes, Joe did talk with Samantha on the phone five times last week for over an hour each. Perhaps there's an innocent explanation. What if these calls were about a major business transaction that had to be handled immediately? What if Joe's been calling her to plan a surprise birthday party for you? You need to think about many possible explanations for Joe's behavior before settling on any one of them. As you do so, try to eliminate both the most naive and most cynical explanations. Give your partner the benefit of the doubt if possible, but don't blind yourself to the truth. Remember that if your partner is having an emotional affair, a clear pattern will emerge that any reasonable person would acknowledge.

PREPARE TO DEAL WITH YOUR PARTNER'S DEFENSIVENESS

Chances are pretty good that your partner's response to your concerns won't be this: "Honey, you're absolutely right. I've been having an emotional affair, and I'm breaking it off this minute." That's just not how people who are engaged in emotional affairs react. Instead, they tend to get defensive. They deny or minimize the situation, justify their actions, blame their partners, and launch angry counterattacks.

Denial: "I'm not having an emotional affair. I don't know what you're talking about. I would never do something like that. You've got it all wrong."

Minimization: "Sure, I'm spending a little extra time with Alan. But it's no big deal. Well, maybe it's a small problem, but I don't see why you're getting so upset about it."

Justification: "Hey, I have the right to spend time with anybody I want. It's only my business what I do and where I go."

Blame: "Yes, I'm spending more and more time with Harry than with you. But you only have yourself to blame. If you were more caring, none of this would be happening."

Counterattack: "What do you mean I'm having an emotional affair? You're the one always talking on the phone with your friends. I'll bet you spend more time jabbering on that phone every day than I spend on the computer with Grace."

So be ready for anything when you confront your partner. Above all, don't let yourself be distracted by these games and ploys. Don't get defensive yourself. Don't get petty or mean. Stay calm and stick to the facts. When your partner realizes that ignoring you, pretending nothing is happening, or huffing and puffing won't deter you, then you can get down to business.

KNOW WHAT YOU WANT TO STOP AND START

Previously we discussed the need to get your facts straight and specific. The same advice applies to telling your partner exactly what you want him or her to stop doing and what you want to start or restart together. You'll need to do better than "Just stop it" and "Let's be nice to each other." Exactly what behavior do you want stopped, and what specific things would you like to start doing to reconnect with each other?

Imagine, for instance, that Hector believes his wife Elena is having an emotional affair with her coworker Rafael. Just saying "Stop it" isn't enough. Elena can't cut off all conversation with Rafael, because they're on the same work crew. But Hector could request that she avoid talking to Rafael during lunch or breaks. He could suggest she refrain from discussing their marital relationship with Rafael. He could ask her to come home after work instead of heading to the bars with Rafael. On a more positive note, Hector could offer to talk to her more often about their emotional relationship. Maybe Elena would like it if he initiated a phone call during the workday just to say hello. Perhaps hugging more often would help them feel safer with each other.

Details are important when you challenge your partner to end an emotional affair. It's absolutely essential that you thoroughly think through your wants and needs before you begin your intervention.

BE WILLING TO COMPROMISE, BUT KNOW YOUR BOTTOM LINE

You'll have to do some soul-searching once you've decided what you want. You need to ask yourself one big question: What is your bottom line? Which of your partner's behaviors are totally unacceptable to you? The bottom line is that you will end the relationship (if not now, then eventually) if your partner won't change these actions. Of course, you must think this through very carefully. Bottom-line demands can be deal breakers, and your relationship is one big deal.

Perhaps right now, you have no bottom-line issues. As much as you dislike your partner's emotional affair, you aren't ready to put the whole relationship at stake just to try to stop it. That's okay. Just be honest with yourself.

Everything but bottom-line issues should be subject to negotiation and compromise. Hector, for example, wants Elena to avoid taking breaks or eating lunch with Rafael. But Elena might argue that breaks are only ten minutes long and that other crew members always join them on break. Hector then might be willing to accept that situation if Elena agreed to stay away from Rafael during lunch.

Beware of two possible mistakes you could make. First, don't treat a negotiable issue as if it were a bottom-line concern. In essence, you'll be bluffing if you do that. Your partner then might call your bluff: "No, I refuse to quit having lunch with Rafael"; and then what will you do? Second, don't accept compromises that make you feel sick inside just to end the conflict. Make sure you really can live with your partner's behavior. If not, you'll regret later what you agreed to. Also, you'll find yourself in a one-down position if you try to get your partner to renegotiate.

PLAN THE DETAILS OF YOUR INITIAL INTERVENTION

You now are almost ready to approach your partner. The last task is to carefully plan out when, where, and how to take this step. You'll need to eliminate certain obvious situations. Avoid any of these three scenes: (1) trying to confront the issue when either of you is under the influence of alcohol or mood-altering chemicals (too risky), (2) confronting your partner in the presence of your rival (which puts your partner in a no-win situation), and (3) challenging your partner in front of family or friends, or in public (too embarrassing). It's usually best to plan for a private meeting with enough time set aside to avoid rushing things. All distractions (television, cell phones, and so on) should be eliminated. Pick a time when neither of you would be sleepy or sick.

Should you have a specific time in mind or just wait for a good opportunity? That's up to you, but we recommend thinking and planning ahead.

Should you let your partner know the topic of conversation in advance? Generally we'd say yes, unless you know that your partner would simply refuse to discuss the matter if forewarned. True, advance notice does give your partner time to build up defenses, but it also lessens the chance that your partner will feel tricked or ambushed.

Should you wait for the perfect time for this encounter? No, because there is no perfect time.

Should you wait until you really have everything in your life under control and are calm, cool, and collected? Not unless you're a very patient individual, because you'll probably have to wait a long time. Plan, but don't overplan. Find a good-enough time, place, and setting. Then go ahead.

We'll describe some important keys to a successful intervention next.

TAKING ACTION

You've prepared carefully for this important meeting with your partner. The following guidelines will increase the odds that this encounter will be productive.

- Be assertive, not aggressive, as you discuss the situation.

- Remember the four *c*'s: be clear, concrete, concise, and controlled.

- Detail how your partner's behavior affects you and your family.

- Seek collaborative (win-win) ways to resolve your differences.

- Share your positive hopes for the future.

- Schedule a follow-up session.

Be Assertive, Not Aggressive, as You Discuss the Situation

Assertive: Saying what you need to say while staying respectful of the other person, asking instead of demanding, remaining civil and polite even when things become emotional, being willing to let the other person speak without immediately interrupting, intending to influence the listener from a position of equality

Aggressive: Demanding instead of requesting, trying to intimidate the other person in order to get what you want, shaming and blaming instead of staying focused on the topic, lecturing instead of discussing, making personality attacks, seeking victory at any cost, intending to control the listener from a position of superiority

It's easy to become aggressive when you try to talk with your partner about his or her emotional affair. After all, this is a highly emotional subject and the stakes are high. Besides, it's quite possible that your partner will react angrily and defensively when you first bring up this topic. Try to remember, though, that successful people usually have the ability to stay calm during a storm. You really won't gain anything if you let things get out of hand. In fact, you might lose a lot. So don't give in to temptation here. Don't swear, threaten, bring up every stupid thing your partner did in the last ten years, make impossible demands, or attack your partner's personality. Instead, stick to your agenda. Stay calm. Stay polite. Stay strong.

The Four C's: Be Clear, Concrete, Concise, and Controlled

"Emmy, I need you to understand that I will not accept your spending an hour every day after work talking with Larry." Nothing is vague here. This is an example of clear communication.

"Leo, I want you to get home by 5:30 so we can have supper together before I take the kids to volleyball practice." This is a concrete statement because Leo's partner says exactly what verifiable behavior she desires from him.

"Sally, we don't have to talk about this forever. All I need is fifteen minutes of your time right now." Sally's partner is prepared to say quickly, without a lot of repetition or confusion, exactly what bothers him.

"Reuben, you can be angry with me if you want. I'm not angry right now. But I do have to insist that you listen to what I've got to say." Reuben's partner refuses to get sucked into a useless fight. That means he'll have to listen to her rather than distract her into an argument.

You might consider writing out the main points you need to make on a sheet of paper or a set of note cards, so you can make sure you say everything you need to say. But on each point, ask yourself if you've written a sentence that's clear, concrete, concise, and controlled. If not, write it out again. If you're still having trouble, try running those sentences by a good friend, a counselor, or another person with whom you've shared your concerns.

Detail How Your Partner's Behavior Affects You and Your Family

Sometimes, in fact frequently, the straying partner doesn't fully realize just how hurtful is his or her behavior. Your partner might be more willing to change this behavior on learning the extent of the damage done. So tell your partner. Let him know that the kids are asking where he is and when he's getting home. Tell her about the hours you've spent worrying about what's going on with her. Describe the times you've had to change plans abruptly because he wasn't where he'd said he'd be. Mention any physical effects you're suffering, such as headaches, sleep problems, and anxiety attacks. Tell your partner if you've started to consider ending the relationship because of the emotional affair. Mention that even your partner's parents are concerned and have even asked you what's wrong with him or her lately. Don't exaggerate. Don't lecture. Don't moralize. Just stick with the real effects of the choices your partner's been making. Hopefully these factual statements will help your partner get past his or her defenses of denial, minimization, and justification and into reality.

Seek Collaborative (Win-Win) Ways to Resolve Your Differences

As you confront your partner, remember that this person is indeed your partner in life. He or she's not the enemy, not an evil person, but someone you love. So don't treat this situation as if it were a war or battle to the death. You'll feel better and probably get farther if you can at least begin negotiations from this approach: "We can find a way to resolve this problem together." Also, keep two goals in mind: (1) to convince your partner to end the emotional affair and (2) to deepen your mutual emotional relationship.

Be firm. Maintain your bottom line. Don't be wishy-washy. But at the same time, stay open to creative solutions that will help both of you feel respected by the end of the discussion.

Here's an example of how two people we'll call Teresa and Steve worked out their differences. First, Teresa laid out everything she knew about Steve's relationship with his friend Karen. She showed him their most recent phone bill, which included thrice-daily calls to Karen. She had written down six different excuses he'd made in the last two weeks for getting home so late. Teresa described how Steve's actions had negatively impacted their relationship by comparing the fun activities they'd had last year with the lack of activities together since Karen entered the picture. Teresa mentioned that she missed Steve's companionship and reminded him that they used to share feelings a lot more frequently than now. Teresa told him she was certain he was having an emotional affair. She told him that it would have to end before she could feel safe again in their partnership.

Steve was initially defensive. He didn't like hearing all those facts because he knew that he couldn't just blow them off. But he tried to minimize the situation, insisting that Karen was just a friend. At first he thought Teresa was accusing him of having a sexual affair, so he spent time trying to prove that he wasn't involved with Karen that way. Teresa had to return several times to her main concern: it was Steve's emotional connection with Karen, not his physical one, that bothered her. Teresa tried to stay calm, although she did let herself cry a couple of times when her feelings temporarily overwhelmed her.

It took two hours of serious discussion before Steve could accept the reality that he was indeed having an emotional affair. But even then, he wasn't ready to agree to have nothing to do with Karen ever again. After all, he argued, he and Karen had been casual friends for a long time before they began this emotional affair. Couldn't they go back to that less-threatening arrangement? But Teresa wanted Steve to curtail all contact with Karen. "How could I trust you not to get overinvolved with her again?" she asked. Fortunately, they eventually did find common ground. Steve would break all contact with Karen (after a brief call to explain why) for at least a month, and then he and Teresa would look at the situation again.

Share Your Positive Hopes for the Future

It's never a good idea just to talk about how to stop bad stuff in a relationship. That mostly leaves partners with a bad taste for what happened and unwillingness to keep talking. Fortunately, Teresa was determined not to let her conversation with Steve end on a totally negative note.

Steve was still obviously unhappy. He'd given up a lot, he thought, and for what? That's when Teresa shifted the subject to how they could improve their relationship. Steve revealed that he believed Teresa didn't care all that much about him because she didn't ask about his work and seldom shared her feelings with him. Teresa recognized some truth in his complaints. But she refused to take the blame for all their emotional distancing. Instead, she proposed several ways she had thought through to improve their partnership. She suggested daily check-ins and a couple of intellectually and emotionally stimulating books they could read together. She suggested the possibility of marriage counseling. Steve agreed to those ideas. He added that he wanted and needed more physical contact as well, both erotic and nonerotic, because touch was very healing for him.

Now Steve could visualize a reason to give up his emotional affair. He could even imagine becoming better friends with Teresa. It was still a stretch to believe he could ever be as emotionally intimate with her as he'd been with Karen. But at least he could look forward to something positive coming out of this difficult situation.

This initial confrontation took almost three hours. It was powerful and emotional. But through all that time, Teresa kept her mind on the two targets of ending the emotional affair and improving their relationship. She didn't treat Steve as an opponent. She kept in mind the goal of having both her and Steve feel that the conversation was productive, respectful, and hopeful.

Schedule a Follow-Up Session

Confronting an emotional affair is painful. That makes it all too easy to have only one conversation about it. Then it's back to silently thinking, "I hope this mess goes away soon." But it won't. Something that takes as long to develop and play out as an emotional affair seldom just disappears. It's not unusual, for example, for the straying partner to promise to cut off contact with the third party, try to do so, but end up still having occasional contact. It's almost as if the straying partner wants to keep the third party in reserve, just in case things go sour again with the committed partner.

Be sure to schedule at least one follow-up session with your partner. That meeting should take place within two weeks. Once again, reserve a time and place where you can talk at length without interruptions.

Here are some agenda items for this session: (1) Has the straying partner kept his or her promise to break off or severely limit contact with the third person? (2) If so, how hard has that been? (3) How hurt, angry, sad, or fearful are you and your partner? (4) What have the two of you done to emotionally deepen your relationship (such as having a couple of really good talks during this period)? (5) What else have you done to get back to enjoying your relationship and appreciating each other? (6) On a scale of 0 to 100, with 0 meaning "I don't trust you as far as I could throw you," and 100 meaning "I fully and absolutely trust you," what score would you give yourselves today and why?

Do not accept any excuses for avoiding this follow-up session. Don't hesitate to schedule as many more sessions as you need. Stop having them, though, when you feel that your partner's emotional affair is completely over, you've reestablished a trusting and loving relationship, and you both regularly share emotions. At that point, you'll want to get the affair behind you so you can focus on the present.

THE AFTERMATH

Let's backtrack a little here. You've just undertaken your initial confrontational conversation with your partner. It's over. You're by yourself now. You'll need to do a few things to take care of yourself, regardless of whether it went poorly or well:

■ Pay attention to your physical and emotional state.

■ Take stock of what happened as objectively as possible.

■ Use your support system.

■ Take time to do some caring things for yourself.

Pay Attention to Your Physical and Emotional State

A confrontation like you've just had is bound to have an effect at a physical level. So please check out what's going on with your body. Begin by noticing your energy level. Do you feel exhausted, exhilarated, or normal? Are you literally shaking? Or have you gone numb so that you don't feel much of anything? Are you hungry or thirsty? Have any of your muscles tightened up because of the stress? Do you have a headache? What about your breathing? Are you taking normal breaths rather than breathing very shallowly or even hyperventilating?

Now let yourself attend to your current emotional state. What emotions do you feel right now? How angry are you—how sad, scared, hurt, relieved, happy, lonely, disgusted, guilty, or ashamed? Just notice these emotions without trying to change or control them. Then check out your emotional intensity level. Do you feel almost overwhelmed by your feelings because they're so strong? Perhaps you've gone the other way and now find yourself unable to feel much at all? If your emotions had a voice, what do you think they'd say to you about your recent discussion?

Perhaps your body and mind are still quite agitated. If so, what do you need to do now, physically and emotionally, to help you relax? Please don't go on to the next step in the book until you've done something simple to help you regain your balance, such as making yourself a warm cup of tea.

Take Stock of What Happened as Objectively as Possible

It's hard to be objective about this extremely emotional situation. Nevertheless, it's important that you try to accurately evaluate what just happened between you and your partner. So put your emotions aside for a few minutes. Become a scientist, carefully analyzing data. Maintain an attitude of absolute neutrality as you recall the scenes from a few minutes or hours ago. Your job here isn't to convince yourself that things went well or poorly. Instead, your task is to understand as clearly as possible exactly what happened.

> You had some definite goals for this conversation with your partner. How many of them were fully achieved? Were some goals partially achieved? Which goals were not advanced at all?

> You wanted to find out whatever you could about your partner's relationship with that other person. What did you discover?

> Did your partner admit to having an emotional affair rather than deny or minimize it?

> What feelings did your partner express during the conversation? Did his or her feelings change from the start to the conclusion of your talk?

> You probably asked your partner to end altogether or drastically curtail the other relationship. Did your partner commit to doing that? If so, how vague or specific were his or her promises?

What specific promises or commitments did you make? Do they still seem fair and reasonable to you? Can you actually keep those promises? Will you keep them?

What complaints did your partner make about you? Did your partner give detailed examples to back up these complaints?

How clearly and calmly did you present your facts and feelings? What could you do differently during the coming follow-up session?

What, if anything, was forgotten, left out, or put off until later?

What positive things happened during this confrontation that give you reasonable hope for the future?

What else happened that's important to remember?

Use Your Support System

Your partner may ask you not to talk about the emotional affair with others. Your partner will say it's nobody else's business and claim that this problem should remain an entirely private matter. He or she will ask you not to even mention it to your family or best friends. There certainly is some wisdom in this request. After all, your relationship is very personal. It could be embarrassing to both of you if people learn about your partner's emotional affair.

There's another side to this picture though. The conversation you just had with your partner has probably affected you powerfully. You really may need to discuss what happened with a few trusted friends or family members. Our main point is that you have a right to make your own decision. Just use your good common sense here. Don't mention it to the local gossip. Don't share your thoughts and feelings with people who will throw fuel on the fire. But if you need to, discuss your situation with discreet people who can listen well and help keep you grounded in reality.

Don't promise your partner that you'll say nothing to anybody if you can't keep that commitment. Instead, try to negotiate a reasonable agreement covering what either of you might disclose to others. Just insist on your right to decide with whom you'll discuss what's going on in your life.

Take Time to Do Some Caring Things for Yourself

You've now spent time dealing with a very painful issue. The focus has been on your relationship, the "us" part of your life. Of course, you need time to process what happened. Take that time. But then, please try to let go of those "us" thoughts for a while. Don't let yourself obsess. Instead, turn your mind to yourself. What could you do in the next twenty-four hours to help you feel more relaxed? What positive things could you think about? Is there something you could throw yourself into that would temporarily get your mind off this whole emotional affair business?

You'll be wise to have a plan for this phase of your journey. For instance, it would help to have in hand tickets to a comedy club, the movies, or a play. It would be a relief to know that a friend will pick you up this evening for coffee at the bookstore. If you prefer to be alone at times like this, have your jogging clothes ready for a run, a distracting mystery ready for reading, or a weekend reservation at a retreat center.

Give yourself twenty-four hours of self-care. Treat yourself kindly during that time. Then you can return to confronting your partner's emotional affair with greater energy and optimism.

Navigating the Stages

Planning Stage

Here are two important ideas from the planning section: (1) identify your bottom-line (nonnegotiable) demands and (2) identify what concerns you're willing to negotiate.

First, think about your bottom line. Which of your partner's behaviors with the third party must absolutely cease? Try to be as specific as you can. Your demand should pass the secret-recorder test. If there were a secret device recording your partner's every moment, could you tell for certain whether the named behavior had ended?

Next, see if you can write down three other behaviors you want your partner to stop doing with the third party or with you (such as disappearing upstairs to the computer room right after supper every evening). These should be negotiable behaviors, meaning that you're willing to talk about them with your partner and reach a compromise if necessary.

Finally, write down three new behaviors you'd like to start or renew between the two of you. Again, be specific.

Action Stage

Perhaps the most critical guideline in the action stage is to bear in mind the four *c*'s: be clear, concrete, concise, and controlled. Here's an important question for your consideration: How will it be difficult for you to stay clear, concrete, concise, and controlled? What might happen that would keep you from this goal?

Have you collected enough data to speak knowledgeably and with authority? If not, you'll want to be patient or do a little more detective work before making your intervention.

How likely are you to become so excited when you try to speak that you won't make sense? If that could happen, what do you need to do to stay as calm as possible?

How emotional do you feel? Which feelings (anger, fear, sadness, and so on) might be so strong that you would become flooded with emotion and unable to speak? You probably need to talk with others before proceeding so you can deal with these emotions in a safer place.

Aftermath Stage

We suggested that you make a plan for what to do after your intervention. Here's a place to do that:

- With whom can you talk soon after the confrontation who'll be supportive and caring?

- What could you do physically that would help you feel strong and centered (such as taking a walk, exercising, or doing yoga)?

- What do you want to avoid doing that wouldn't be good for you to do, especially when you're emotionally vulnerable (for example, going out drinking, binge eating, and so on)?

- Where will you go after your intervention to gain some time for solitude and reflection if you need it?

- What else do you need to do to help yourself during the aftermath stage?

6

Are You Having an Emotional Affair?

$\mathcal{Y}$our partner has just handed you this book on emotional affairs and expects you to read it and discuss it with him or her. But why? What's that got to do with you? Obviously, your partner thinks you're having an emotional affair. Or perhaps he or she believes that you aren't involved in an emotional affair yet but are moving in that direction. One purpose of this chapter is to help you determine whether or not you're having an emotional affair. Another is to help you decide what to do about it if that's your situation.

Let's begin with a quick review (in case you've begun with this chapter instead of the beginning of the book). *An emotional affair is an intense, primarily emotional, nonsexual relationship that diminishes at least one person's emotional connection with his or her committed partner.* Here are the key elements:

Intensity: A strong attraction to the third party. This person feels very special and important.

Primarily emotional: The relationship with this friend centers on sharing emotions.

Nonsexual: If there's erotic interest, it isn't acted upon.

Diminished emotional connection with your partner: Emotional affairs damage your primary relationship by reducing commitment, emotional sharing, and trust.

GETTING HONEST WITH YOURSELF

Are you having an emotional affair? We're going to ask you to answer some questions to help you find out. But before you do so, please read the next couple of paragraphs carefully.

Nobody likes being accused of doing something damaging. That's why people develop powerful defenses against admitting the meaning of their actions. Four of the most common defenses about emotional affairs are denial, minimization, justification, and blaming your partner. Here are some examples of each:

Denial: "I'm totally innocent. I never had an emotional affair. I'm not having one now."

Minimization: "Well, yes, we've gotten a little too close, but it's really not a big deal."

Justification: "Yeah, I'm having an emotional affair, but it's because of..."

Blaming your partner: "It's all because of you that I needed someone else to talk with."

Please realize that you've got a lot to lose. Your long-term relationship or marriage, the one you've made a serious commitment to, could be at risk. It's critically important for you to face the truth, whatever it is, to save and improve that relationship. You need to be totally honest with yourself. Don't deny, minimize, justify, or blame. Just answer the following questions to the best of your ability.

After you answer the questions, please share your responses with your partner. Try to stay open to honest discussion, again without getting defensive. Remember that your partner is concerned about what's happening because he or she loves you and doesn't want to lose you. The two of you may disagree about some of your answers. Both of you need to rely upon real data in these situations. Can your partner back up that "yes" by reminding you of a specific occasion during which you acted that way? Can you defend your "no" with clear examples? Could the best answer be "sometimes yes and no"?

⌐ The Emotional Affair Questionnaire ⌐

The terms used in this questionnaire are as follows: "Partner" means the marital or relationship partner with whom you've made a long-term commitment. "Friend" means the person with whom you may be having an emotional affair.

Please answer these yes or no questions to the best of your ability based on your recent and current experiences with your friend. (Note: This quiz has not been scientifically tested for validity and reliability, and should only be used as a general guide that could help you better understand your behavior.)

I am more likely to tell my friend what bothers me than my partner.	____ Yes	____ No
I would prefer having lunch or dinner with my friend than my partner.	____ Yes	____ No
My friend has told me secrets even his or her partner doesn't know.	____ Yes	____ No
I have thoughts of leaving my partner for my friend.	____ Yes	____ No
I'm amazed at how well my friend understands me.	____ Yes	____ No
I'm amazed at how well I can understand my friend.	____ Yes	____ No
Sometimes it seems as if my friend and I can read each other's minds.	____ Yes	____ No

My friend seems different from anybody else ____ Yes ____ No
I've ever met.

I put my friend on a pedestal as if he or she ____ Yes ____ No
has no faults.

All my troubles seem to vanish when I'm ____ Yes ____ No
around my friend.

My friend meets emotional needs my ____ Yes ____ No
partner doesn't meet.

Sharing feelings with my friend is more ____ Yes ____ No
important to me than my physical attrac-
tion to him or her.

I get angry or defensive if my partner ques- ____ Yes ____ No
tions my friendship.

I've given up even trying to get my emo- ____ Yes ____ No
tional needs met with my partner.

If I had met my friend before I became ____ Yes ____ No
committed to my partner, I would certainly
have chosen him or her.

I feel empty, lonely, or desperate when I ____ Yes ____ No
can't contact my friend.

I feel guilty about my relationship with my ____ Yes ____ No
friend.

Something would be ruined if I had sex ____ Yes ____ No
with my friend.

Knowing that I'm really important to my ____ Yes ____ No
friend makes me feel special.

The term "emotional affair" seems to fit my ____ Yes ____ No
friendship.

Results:

Give yourself one point for each "yes" response.

0–3 points: You probably are not having an emotional affair.

4–7 points: Borderline—this relationship is more than a normal friendship. You need to ask yourself where you're heading.

8–14 points: You are definitely having an emotional affair, one that is a distinct threat to your committed relationship.

15–20 points: You are totally involved in an emotional affair, one that is certainly heavily damaging your committed relationship.

THE COSTS OF YOUR EMOTIONAL AFFAIR

You might be thinking that your partner is making a huge fuss over a little problem. If that's the case, you're minimizing the situation. An emotional affair is a serious threat to any long-term relationship. Emotional affairs cause damage that can take months to repair. They can even destroy a relationship. The key to understanding why that's true is to think about the word "committed."

Two feet in—that's what it means to be committed to your partner and to your relationship. But that's not what you're doing. You've got one foot in and one foot out. You're taking much of your energy, love, responsibility, and joy out of the circle of mutual caring. You're giving part of your heart to a third person. No wonder your partner feels left out. Of course your partner worries that pretty soon you might take both feet out of the circle.

Your lack of commitment is probably obvious to everybody but you. You're spending less time with your partner and family than before. You decline to talk about anything that really matters. You get irritable if you have to stay home or can't talk to that special friend of yours. You've become thoughtless and forgetful about things like your partner's birthday or career. You're reluctant to tell your partner where you've been or where you're going. You're becoming more and more critical of your partner, if only so you have an excuse to get away. You have become a mystery to your partner and family, and an open book to an outsider.

You just aren't all here. Or rather, you're only half here. And that's not enough. Half of your time, energy, and commitment is way short of what your partner wants and deserves. Would you want and deserve anything less if it were you in this situation?

Is this what you want? How comfortable are you with one foot in and one foot out? Most important, what would it take (inside you) to put that missing foot back into your primary relationship?

About now, you may be thinking about bargaining. Maybe you could somehow maintain your emotional affair while recommitting to your main relationship. Yes, you could do that—if you had three feet! Otherwise, no, that just doesn't work. The only way to get both feet back in is to end your emotional affair. There's no middle way. There's no compromise. You cannot fully commit to your partner while keeping that third party in reserve. You can't hedge your bets.

So here's the bottom line: you must end your emotional affair—now. That's the only way you can make a real, sustained commitment to your true partner in life.

ENDING THE EMOTIONAL AFFAIR

It's time to close your emotional affair. You probably don't want to take this step. You may feel sad, mad, and scared all at once. There's no middle road though. The only way you can return to your main relationship with real energy is to quit what distracts you from it. We've provided two steps to help you carry out this necessary task.

Summon the Courage to Do What It Takes

It's gut-check time. You've gotten yourself into a messy situation, and only you can get out of it. But to do so, you must find the strength to end this emotional affair. This is no time for self-pity.

It's certainly okay to feel sad, but don't grieve as if someone were dying. Feel angry if you must, but don't take it out on your partner. And don't let yourself become paralyzed with fear about ending the emotional affair. Instead, use your emotions to do what you need to do. Feel sad about what you've lost with your partner so you can commit to retrieving that relationship. Get angry enough at yourself to jump into action. Even your fear can be useful here. Use it to remember what it felt like when you and your partner felt safe with each other.

Don't stall around, hoping somehow that you can find a way to maintain your emotional affair. That will only make it harder to end it. This is your time for action.

It's vital that you not delude yourself into thinking that you can maintain a friendship with the person with whom you've been having the emotional affair. It won't work. You'd end up feeling like a compulsive gambler trying to keep to a twenty-five-dollar spending limit at the casino. That gambler will spend everything he or she's got. And you'll end up sharing all your emotions with your friend instead of your real partner.

Make a Plan and Carry It Out

Don't just rush to the phone. You need to think clearly and carefully before you act. Find a good way to end this emotional relationship as cleanly as possible. Make a short and simple plan to end the emotional affair and then carry it out.

What should you say to the person with whom you've been having the emotional affair? Three things: (1) You realize that you've been neglecting your primary relationship by spending so much time and energy with him or her, (2) you've decided to recommit to your primary relationship, and (3) therefore, you must curtail all unnecessary contact with him or her.

You don't have to be mean or cold to this friend with whom you've shared so many important emotions. You do need to be firm though. This is no time to be wishy-washy. You must make a clear statement that you are ending your emotional relationship with him or her.

What about guilt? You'll probably feel bad about abruptly ending the emotional affair. You may fear that you're hurting your friend. You need to take a long-term view to deal with these feelings. Yes, you're causing some pain right now. But this is necessary pain. It extricates you, your friend, and your partner from a no-win situation.

One more thing: Ask yourself how you might sabotage your goal. How could you wind up not ending the emotional affair during your meeting? For example, might you get cold feet at the moment of truth and not say anything? Or might you feel so bad that you'd agree to meet on the sly with this person and hope your partner won't catch on? You'd better come up with a way to counter these tendencies before the meeting. Otherwise you'll blow it.

Now carry out the plan. Keep the discussion short and simple. Avoid arguing with your friend. Don't try to convince him or her that you're doing the right thing. Don't explain, explain, explain. Above all, don't get into a lengthy emotional talk; that's exactly what you're committing to stopping. The idea is to deliver your news and leave the scene.

Should you meet with this person face to face? Yes, but only if you can do so and keep to the plan. If not, you may have to send an e-mail or leave a phone message. What is critical here is for you to terminate the emotional affair quickly and definitively.

RECOMMITTING TO YOUR PRIMARY RELATIONSHIP PARTNER

The next step to truly ending your emotional affair is to deeply and honestly recommit to your primary relationship partner. You need to make and keep this pledge:

> I, _____ [your name], promise to return my energy, emotions, time, and communications to you, _____ [your partner's name]. I pledge to come to you with my concerns. I will do everything I can to help make our relationship mutually loving, caring, and respectful. I have ended my relationship

with _____ [third party's name] so that I can keep this promise. From this point forward, my commitment is to you and only you.

What if you feel you simply cannot make or keep this promise? Well, then you're in trouble. You still only have one foot in. Not only that, but your other foot wants to start walking away. Don't let it though. If you go running off again, you'll only perpetuate your problem. Instead, drag that other foot into the circle any way you can. Remember, it's your foot. It's your choice. You can recommit to your partner now, even while you feel anxious, confused, and ambivalent. Don't wait to make this pledge until you're 100 percent sure you want to. The idea is to make this pledge now so that you can become more deeply committed to working on your primary relationship.

It's no use making this pledge quietly to yourself when nobody's listening. That's just a way to hedge your bet. You need to say it out loud to your partner.

There's one hitch though. You really need to keep this promise once you make it. If you cheat and recontact the third party, you'll lose whatever credibility you have left.

DEALING WITH YOUR SENSE OF LOSS

The immediate urgency for action will be reduced once you end the emotional affair. Then you can take some time to deal with the pain you'll undoubtedly experience. It's perfectly normal for you to feel sad about ending such an intense and rewarding connection. Just keep reminding yourself that you're doing so for a good reason, namely, to save your primary relationship. You'll also want to improve that bond, if at all possible. Oddly, the way to begin is to take a close look at why you got into the emotional affair.

In chapter 3 we discussed how people involved in emotional affairs want something emotionally important to them that they feel is missing from their primary relationships. We identified many of these wants:

I want more emotional connection.

I want more understanding.

I want more praise and less criticism.

I want more freedom.

I want more action.

I want more emotional intensity.

I want more respect.

I want more of the five *a*'s: attention, appreciation, acceptance, admiration, and affirmation.

I want to feel more important and special.

I want more loving friendship (*agape*).

Take a long look at this list of wants and needs. Go back and read chapter 3 to get more information about these emotional desires. Then try to identify the ones that strike home the most for you. These will be the emotional needs that (1) you felt were missing (or weren't present often enough) in your primary relationship and (2) you tried to get met with someone outside your home. And these are exactly the emotional desires you most need to get met within your primary relationship.

So go ahead and grieve the end of your emotional affair. More accurately, grieve the reality that you can't go to that third party to get some of your emotional needs met. But then bring those emotional desires back into your main partnership. Give yourself a new goal: to learn how to get these emotional needs satisfied within your primary relationship and with your true partner.

BRING YOUR EMOTIONAL SELF BACK TO YOUR PRIMARY RELATIONSHIP

Make it your goal to get both feet in. To get two feet in means completely returning yourself emotionally to your partner. Now that might take a while to happen. It may be a gradual process. But don't dawdle. Don't hold yourself back because of anger at your partner, fear of closeness, sadness at the loss of your other relationship, or guilt about how you strayed.

How do you return fully to your committed relationship? First, start talking a lot. Most important, share your feelings with your partner. Tell him or her when you feel glad, sad, mad, scared, lonely, guilty, or ashamed. That may take courage when you begin, but it'll get easier every time you open up (especially, of course, when your partner listens with caring to what you say). Next, invite your partner to share his or her feelings with you. When your partner does this, make sure you respond with interest and concern rather than advice and criticism. Third, make a conscious decision to trust your partner. Think of your partner as your ally and friend, someone who wants the best for you. Then flip that idea around and make a conscious decision to be trustworthy yourself.

You've now identified at least some of the emotional wants and needs you felt weren't getting met in your primary relationship. This is the time to tell your partner about them. Then the two of you can discuss together how you can get those needs met within the relationship.

Only you can really know whether you have both feet back in. Only you can tell if you even want to put them there. But here's one way to help make it happen. Every morning when you arise, renew your commitment to full involvement. Ask yourself what you can do today to reinvest in your partnership. Then, at the end of the day, ask yourself how you did. Were you able to stay connected mentally, physically, and emotionally? If so, great. If not, what kept you from that goal? See if you can figure out what slowed you down so you can make a stronger commitment tomorrow morning.

Please remember the bottom line: to retrieve your primary relationship, you must relinquish your emotional affair.

Deal with the Guilt of Abandoning Your Emotional Affair Partner

You may be having difficulty ending your emotional affair because of guilt. Perhaps you're worried that quitting now will hurt the person with whom you've forged such an intimate relationship. And, frankly, that may be true. It might help you, though, to keep these points in mind:

- Your emotional affair partner is an adult who can take care of himself or herself. You don't need to feel responsible for making this person happy or meeting his or her needs.

- You have to end this emotional affair quickly and cleanly so you can fully recommit to your primary relationship.

- Life is hard. Sometimes you must cause pain to people you care about. That's reality.

- It's time for a chapter in each of your lives to end so you can start another chapter.

- In the long run, you'll feel guiltier if you don't end this emotional affair than if you keep it going. You'll just keep damaging everybody in your life, including your emotional affair partner.

- The bottom line: you can't have it both ways. You must give up your emotional affair for the sake of your primary relationship.

Which of these statements actually helps you? Can you think of something else you can say to yourself that will help you handle your guilt about ending your emotional affair?

Are You a "Third Party"?

You may be having an emotional affair with a partner who is also in a committed relationship. Both of you choose to confide in each other instead of your partners. That means that both of you are cheating (emotionally) on your partners. Each of you is weakening your primary relationship. At least two people (your committed partner and your emotional affair partner's spouse), and maybe several more family members, are getting hurt because of your actions. This is all the more reason to end your emotional affair immediately.

Here are several questions we'd like you to think about:

How do you feel about being a third party?

What would happen if you ran into your emotional affair partner's spouse? If you did, could you really open up and talk freely with that person about your relationship with his or her partner? Or would you feel awkward and just want to get away as fast as you could?

How often have you thought about the effects of your emotional affair on that individual?

How bad do you feel about the effects of your emotional affair on him or her?

You can take action now to quit being a third party. Are you willing to do so?

7

A Couple's Guideline for Recovering from an Emotional Affair

*T*he emotional affair is over. One of you broke it off and renewed your commitment to your primary partner. But that doesn't mean all is well. Both of you are still hurting. The bridge of trust between you has been damaged, and it'll take a while to repair it. The good news is that once that structure is rebuilt, it actually will be stronger than ever before. To make that happen, though, each of you will need to work hard.

There are so many questions that need to be answered: "Is the emotional affair really over?" "What happened?" "Why did it happen?" "How did it happen?" "What now?" "How do we get back to a normal life?" "Is it possible to forgive?" "Does my partner love me?" "Does my partner trust me?" "How can I regain that lost love and trust?" "How much should we talk about it?" "How can we make sure this doesn't happen again?" Try to be patient. The answers to many of these questions will emerge gradually. Have faith that over time the two of you can work your way through them.

In chapter 4 we mentioned that it's important to keep your focus on the "us" in your relationship, not the "me" or the "you." This is particularly true now that the emotional affair has ended. This is your opportunity to deepen and enrich your mutual love, caring, and commitment.

The guidelines that follow will help the two of you rebuild your trust, answer the preceding questions, and develop your "us" connection.

REPAIRING YOUR RELATIONSHIP ONE ROOM AT A TIME

Imagine that a loving relationship is like a well-built eight-room house. However, the names of the rooms in this house aren't kitchen, living room, and so on. They are trust, commitment, friendship, love, respect, acceptance, forgiveness, and growth. That emotional affair was like a powerful storm that blew so ferociously that it almost destroyed your house. Fortunately, though, your home survived. Unfortunately, each room has taken some significant damage. So now the two of you must get to work rebuilding each room. Of course, this would also be a good time to think not only about repairing the destruction but also actually improving the appearance of those rooms. Why settle for what you had when you can do a little needed remodeling?

Let's inspect each room separately to see what could be done.

Trust

Probably the room that needs the most immediate attention is trust. Think of the emotional affair as a kind of unattractive mold that has spread over the walls, ceiling, floors, and furniture in this room. Every lie, half-truth, and omission either of you told spread the mold. Now the two of you need to grab some strong disinfectant and start scrubbing away. Can you guess the name of the disinfectant? It's called "honesty." You need the most powerful type, by the way; it's name is "absolute honesty." That doesn't mean you should be mean or brutal, however. You can be both honest and tactful. You can be both frank and caring. What matters is telling the truth. For example, if you were the strayer, don't say that you never think of the third party. That bird just won't fly. It's better to admit that you think of him or her frequently (and then reassure your partner that you are here to stay). Or, if you're the betrayed partner, don't say that you've forgiven your partner completely when you're still full of anger and doubt.

However, before you ask a potentially painful or difficult question of your partner, first ask yourself this question: how important is this concern? For instance, does it actually matter how many phone calls your partner made in the month of September to your rival? Why do you need to know that particular piece of information? Don't waste time and energy on useless questions.

Also, don't ask questions only designed to make the partner who strayed feel bad. He or she probably feels bad enough already.

Commitment

This room doesn't look so bad right now. Above all, you're both in it. Either of you could be long gone, but you aren't. Instead, you've decided to stick it out. That says a lot.

You'll probably need to spend a fair amount of time together in this room. In the previous chapter, we wrote about the need to put both feet into the circle of your partnership. That idea applies to both of you. Each of you must affirm your commitment to your partner and to the relationship. Furthermore, you'll need to do so out loud and frequently as you begin this reconciliation process.

There's one piece of furniture you'll want to add to this room: a full-length mirror. Stand in front of it together, holding hands. That will help you recapture the feeling of belonging, the sense of deep connection that makes your relationship worth keeping.

Friendship

John Gottman, the great marriage researcher, writes: "Happy marriages are based on a deep friendship. By this, I mean a mutual respect for and enjoyment of each other's company.... Friendship fuels the flames of romance because it offers the best protection against feeling adversarial toward your spouse" (Gottman and Silver 1999, 19–20). So, in the long run, this room will be the equivalent of your living room, the place where you can really relax and enjoy each other's company. And, wonderfully, there's no room more solid than one built on a foundation of friendship.

The recent emotional affair almost certainly damaged your friendship. You may have even begun treating each other more like enemies than friends. Perhaps you're still doing that. If so, it's time to stop the nasty stuff and restart your friendship. Just as a reminder, friends...

...are kind to each other.

...do things to help each other feel good.

...want good things for each other.

...share important thoughts, feelings, yearnings, and goals with each other.

...think of each other frequently, even when apart.

...spend time together.

...like one another.

...enjoy being with each other.

...feel safe when together.

...say nice things about each other to others.

...feel as if they want to go through life with each other.

You can begin to deepen your friendship just by reviewing this list. Notice any of those items that are partly or completely missing from your relationship. Then discuss together, without blaming or becoming defensive, how you can add them to your partnership. For example, it's not unusual right now to feel unsafe with each other. But don't let your fears keep you apart. Instead, look for ways you do feel relatively safe with each other. Discuss how that happens by asking yourselves what you're doing right during those times. Keep doing whatever has been working. Then take that information into new situations so you can feel safe together everywhere you go.

Love

If love really were a room in a house, it would be one whose furniture and decorations you frequently change. That's because loving someone isn't a static thing. During good times, love grows and changes as you go from initial attraction to courtship, early marriage, child rearing, and so on. Then again, hard times sometimes diminish feelings of love. Recently, because of the pain around the emotional affair, you may have even wondered whether you actually still love your partner.

Fortunately, there are three ways the two of you can address the need to renew your loving feelings. The first is to tell each other in many ways that you love each other. For instance, you can hold hands, look deeply into your partner's eyes, and share your loving words. Or you can express your love nonverbally, with hugs and caresses. You could even write a love letter to your partner.

A second way to be more loving is to show your love. You can do this by making time to be with each other, listening carefully with a real desire to understand your partner, and keeping your promise to come to your partner to share your feelings before going to anyone else.

The third approach for deepening feelings of love is to take in each other's caring. This may be difficult right now since you both may feel emotionally injured. It's easy to doubt your partner's sincerity when you're trying to get over feeling betrayed. You may need to relearn how to take in your partner's love just a little bit at a time. Try to remember that every couple goes through rough periods but love perseveres. Your goal is for the two of you to repair your relationship. That can only happen when you accept the kind words and deeds your partner offers, including professions of love.

If you think that this room has been pretty badly damaged, we suggest you read our book *Reclaim Your Relationship: A Workbook of Exercises and Techniques to Help You Reconnect with Your Partner* (John Wiley & Sons, Inc., 2006).

Respect

It's all too easy to blame and shame each other when one of you has had an emotional affair. That's when partners say things like this: "What's wrong with you? Are you an idiot?" "You're so selfish you don't care about anybody other than yourself." "You're always trying to control me; that's your problem." While statements like these say a lot about the amount of pain you're in, they're disrespectful. Unfortunately, they don't help repair your relationship at a time when repair is desperately needed. You both need to replace this disrespectful pattern with a more respectful attitude. Here are a few guidelines to help you do that:

- Begin each day with a promise to respect your partner's dignity.

- Make sure you notice your partner's positive words and actions.

- Give your partner praise rather than criticism. Consciously try to give at least five times more praise than criticism.

- Remember that real respect for your partner is about appreciating him or her as a human being.

We're not suggesting that this is easy to do. It's difficult, because by now you've probably been angry and frustrated with each other for a long time. But you've got to take this step if you want your relationship to get better. If not, it really won't matter that the emotional affair has ended, because you'll both carry on as if it were still going on.

Acceptance

Have you ever wondered why the famous Serenity Prayer begins "God, grant me the serenity to accept the things I cannot change,..." before it continues "...the courage to change the things I can..."? We think it's because the universe is filled with many, many more things human beings cannot change than things they can.

If acceptance were a room in your home, it would probably be filled with big, bulky pieces of furniture that are only moved with great difficulty. These represent all the things your partner keeps doing that you'd like to stop. You can keep trying to move those bulky pieces of furniture forever. Maybe it's better to just let them stay where they are and walk around them when they seem to be in the way.

Accepting people as they are is just the opposite of demanding that they think, speak, and act exactly as you'd prefer. Instead, acceptance means learning to let people be the way they are. That means giving up trying to make a morning person into a night person, a live-for-the-moment free spirit into someone who plans carefully for the future, or a highly emotional person into a rational thinking machine. Minimally, partners must tolerate their differences even if that means taking deep breaths and keeping their mouths shut. Better yet is to really appreciate those differences. That happens when partners realize that they can learn new ways to deal with life from their partners. And better still is encouraging your partner's differences. One example would be for a nonreligious partner to encourage his or her devoutly religious spouse to attend a church retreat.

All that's fairly general though. There's something more immediate the two of you have to find a way to accept: the reality that one of you has had an emotional affair. (Just to clarify, we're definitely not saying that you should accept an ongoing affair. There are some bottom-line issues that cannot be tolerated in a committed relationship.) This affair might have shattered the belief that neither of you would ever do something that would cause so much pain to your partner and threaten the relationship itself. But it has happened. It cannot be denied. It must be accepted. It's a piece of furniture that can never be removed from your house. However, how you go about dealing with the emotional affair is critical. One way will turn it into a bulky, ugly, smelly hulk. The other way will let it have a smaller and cleaner feel. The first way is resentment. The second is forgiveness.

Forgiveness

Here's a thorough definition of forgiveness: "Forgiveness is a willingness to abandon one's right to resentment… toward one who unjustly injured us, while fostering the undeserved qualities of compassion, generosity, and even love toward him or her" (Enright, Freedman, and Rique 1998, 46–7). Let's break down that definition in the light of an emotional affair.

First, "a willingness to abandon one's right to resentment": Yes, each of you has a right to deeply resent your partner. One of you broke faith by turning your emotional life away from your partner and toward another. And one of you got really upset about that and insisted that the emotional affair had to end. Either of you could nurse your anger for days, weeks, months, or years. The trouble is that the longer you hold on to your resentment, the stronger it will become. Not only will that particular piece of furniture look uglier and uglier over time, but also you won't be able to take your eyes off of it.

Are you ready to begin letting go of your resentment, even though you have every right to hang on to it?

The second part of the definition of forgiveness is "fostering the undeserved qualities of compassion, generosity, and even love toward him or her." That means taking your partner back into your heart. It means choosing to feel what Buddhists call "loving-kindness" toward your partner.

Notice the mention of the word "undeserved" in the definition. Your partner cannot earn your forgiveness, not even by forgoing the emotional affair. Nobody ever earns forgiveness. Rather, it's something you choose to give, no strings attached, because you're ready in your heart to reconnect at the deepest level of human bonding.

Don't think of forgiveness as a one-time event. It's a process that takes time and effort. You might think you've forgiven your partner, only to wake up one morning full of resentment once again. Complete forgiveness is possible, though, if you can be patient with yourself and your partner (but only if the emotional affair is really over).

Growth

True, a powerful storm almost destroyed your house. But now that you're rebuilding, why not add a new room or two? Take a minute to think about what you want in that addition. Perhaps it could be a room for deeper spiritual or religious involvement. Or maybe you could use a recreation room where the two of you could play. How about a place to keep sharing your feelings now that you have a good start along those lines? You might even need an "adults only" room for certain private events.

You two are the architects. So design that new room together. Then figure out what you need to do to build it.

DOS AND DON'TS FOR RECONNECTING

Dos and Don'ts for Healing After an Emotional Affair	
DO...	**DON'T...**
Have hope for the future.	Give up.
Talk about the emotional affair.	Rehash endlessly.
Notice and share your feelings.	Let feelings dominate thought.
Take responsibility for your own actions.	Blame your partner for your choices.
Choose to trust.	Be naive or paranoid.
Invite your partner back into your life.	Demand total connection.
Relax and start returning to normal.	Run away from the issues.
Start exploring what's been missing.	Try to fix everything at once.

Healing from an emotional affair is seldom quick or easy for either partner. However, the preceding list of dos and don'ts will help you get through this troubling time with less pain and discomfort. Take a look at these helpful and unhelpful ways to discuss the emotional affair. Try to follow the guidelines at all times, but especially when you're most tempted to say or do something particularly nasty to your mate. Do the best you can, even though sometimes it will be difficult. Remember, the idea is to get closer over time, not to drive each other away.

Have Hope for the Future

Yes, it's hard not to give up hope for the future after all you've been through. But you've probably gone through worse in your life: deaths, illnesses, divorce or relationship breakups, financial disasters, or religious or spiritual crises. Some of these you've handled alone, others with your partner. You are tough inside. Your relationship has many strengths. So stay hopeful. You two will find a way to get through this mess together. Hopefully, you'll even emerge with a deeper, more satisfying connection than before the emotional affair developed.

Talk About the Emotional Affair

Here's what we've seen frequently in this situation. The straying partner feels guilty, ashamed, and stupid about what he or she's done. All this partner wants to do is apologize one time and never talk about it again. Meanwhile, the committed partner has many questions, concerns, worries, and doubts and thus needs to talk a lot about the emotional affair. So try to keep in mind these two realities. To the strayer: Talking about what happened one time is never enough. You just can't threaten the integrity of your relationship and expect your partner to be cool with it just because you're back. To the committed partner: Talking about the emotional affair a thousand times will never be enough. You'll always have more questions and concerns (or the need to ask the same question yet again). At some point you'll have to stop asking those questions, even though you still aren't completely satisfied with the answers.

You'll both need to compromise and be flexible. That means, if you're the strayer, you must often be willing, even if far from eager, to keep talking about what happened, because your partner needs to talk about it. But, if you're the committed partner, it also means that you must not endlessly ask the same questions. Sometimes you'll just have to keep quiet, if only out of compassion for your partner's discomfort.

Notice and Share Your Feelings

Mutually sharing your feelings is essential for healing your relationship. After all, the core behavior during an emotional affair is that the strayer shares emotions with the third party but not with his or her committed partner. So becoming willing, and even eager, to share feelings with each other changes everything. It allows an intimate connection, perhaps deeper than before.

Heed one caution: If misused, sharing emotions can be very hurtful. One danger is talking about your feelings too often and too repetitively. For example, it really doesn't help to tell your partner over and over how sad you felt when he or she wouldn't talk with you. But it's just as damaging to become so emotional as you talk that you can no longer think. That's when you'll say things you'll soon regret. Try to maintain a balance between feelings and thoughts. That means that, if you're already quite emotionally inclined, you'll need to make every effort to stay fairly calm when talking about the emotional affair. On the other hand, if you're a very analytic individual, you'll need to make a definite effort to notice and share your feelings.

There's one more thing to remember about emotions. An emotion is your personal reaction to someone's behavior. The emotion is not caused by your partner's actions, so don't hold your partner responsible for "making" you sad, mad, scared, or lonely. The idea is to confront your partner's unacceptable behavior while attending to your feelings.

Take Responsibility for Your Actions Without Blaming

If we were to name the single sentence we least like hearing when counseling couples, it would be "You made me do it." It's not unusual, for example, for the strayer to blame the committed partner for his or her involvement with another. "If you were more loving, if you'd paid me more attention, if you were nicer, if you'd listened better, then I never would've had this emotional affair." That's a lot of baloney. Your partner didn't make you have that emotional affair. You chose it. Don't try to transfer the guilt for what you've done. It will only make things worse.

This is big. You both must avoid the blame and shame game. And the only way to do that is for each of you to take full responsibility for the bad choices and poor decisions you've made. These may have included secret meetings, nasty phone calls, name calling, screaming and yelling, and general meanness. Whatever happened during this terrible time can be put behind you, but only when you take full responsibility for everything you've said and done.

Choose to Trust

Previously in this chapter we mentioned that rebuilding trust is an absolutely essential element in your recovery as a couple. Here, it's useful to describe two kinds of mistakes you could make in this area.

The first error is to be too trusting. This is particularly important for the committed partner. Please don't be so gullible and naive as to believe that your partner would never contact the third party again. This may be the case. Your partner did promise to end the emotional affair, didn't he or she? But promises are sometimes broken, especially when the two of you are just beginning to reconcile. It's perfectly reasonable to keep your eyes open. It's okay to ask a few questions about your partner's actions and intentions. Your partner has to re-earn your trust rather than expect you to just give it away.

Just don't get paranoid. Don't take on the role of a private detective or, worse, a district attorney out to prove that your partner is cheating again. You'll become consumed by the job, totally obsessed and insecure. Besides, you can't stop your partner if he or she really wants to maintain the emotional affair. Your partner will find a way. But chances are pretty good that you'll find out what he or she's up to soon enough. You'll know something's happening because your partner will once again start drifting away.

Be reasonably trusting. Believe what your partner says unless you have good reason to doubt. But if you do become suspicious, then bring your concerns to the table. Tell your partner what you disbelieve and ask for an explanation.

Invite Your Partner Back into Your Life

You two have been emotionally isolated for a while. Now is the time to reconnect. That means talking a lot, sharing feelings, going places together, having fun, and quite possibly rekindling your sex life. We advise you to make time every day for meaningful contact. Don't overdo it though. You won't want to fix one problem (excessive distancing) by creating another (overinvolvement).

It's tempting to deal with your insecurities by trying to become joined at the hip. That way you can keep a constant eye on each other so that nobody strays. However, after a few days or weeks like this, one or both of you will feel smothered. You'll need to get away. And that's good. You can't build a trusting relationship based on the fear of being apart. Each of you must let the other go out into the world so you can learn whether your partner will come back to you voluntarily.

Practice moderation here. Aim for creating good, solid, daily contact based on the joy of reconnection rather than fear-based symbiosis.

Relax and Start Returning to Normal

When will this crisis be over? When can life return to normal? You've probably been losing sleep, feeling anxious or depressed, and maybe getting sick as your immune system becomes overburdened from stress. You both need this huge, messy ordeal to end as soon as possible.

If your relationship is starting to mend, then try to relax a little. Tell yourself it's okay to quit worrying so much. Get back to (or start) your exercise program to burn off some energy. Develop some soothing routines with your partner, such as morning coffee or a daily stroll.

Our warning here: don't make getting back to normal such a high priority that you quit dealing with the emotional affair. You must allow time and opportunity to explore what went wrong in your relationship and how to fix it. You need to strike a flexible balance between "Thank God, that's over and done with" and "Yes, but there are still plenty of things we need to discuss."

Start Exploring What's Been Missing

In chapter 3 we noted a list of unmet wants and needs that sometimes lead people to begin an emotional affair. But it's not just the straying partner who has unmet wants and needs in a troubled relationship. Both of you are probably hungry to be better nurtured by your partner. So please review chapter 3 together. Try to do this cooperatively and nondefensively. Look at all the wants and needs that are described. Identify which wants are most important to work on. Begin from this premise: if either of you has an unmet need in your relationship, it hurts both of you. Therefore make it your goal to better meet each other's strongest wants and needs.

Prioritize; don't immediately attempt to meet each and every unmet want. That's just too much. You'll experience too many failures and get discouraged. Also, don't hurry. Focus on steadily improving your connections over time. Gradual changes last longer than instant ones. The idea here is to set new goals for your partnership without becoming totally overwhelmed.

BECOMING HELPMATES AND BEST FRIENDS

We believe that the strongest and most enduring relationships are those in which the two partners are both helpmates and best friends to each other. A helpmate is someone who can be relied on to carry approximately half the burdens of the partnership, such as raising the children, bringing in an income, developing social connections, and so on. Who does what varies with each couple, of course. But most satisfied partnerships are ones in which life's responsibilities are shared pretty equally.

Becoming and staying best friends is at least as important as being helpmates in today's relationships. And the friendship is exactly what is endangered or destroyed when one partner has an emotional affair. The point of this chapter, and indeed of this entire book, is that emotional affairs greatly damage trust between partners. True friendship depends on trust, and trust is broken during emotional affairs.

The Current State of Your Relationship Home

Imagine that your relationship really does resemble a house. Please take a good look at the shape it's in.

1. What about the general structure? How does it look from the outside? Does your home seem pretty well built? Are there a few cracks here and there? Or does it look as if it's ready to fall to pieces any minute?

2. Now head inside. Take a careful view of each of the eight rooms: trust, commitment, friendship, love, respect, acceptance,

forgiveness, and growth. Which ones need the most immediate attention? Which are in better shape?

3. Do you think your partner agrees with your opinions? Ask him or her to go through the rooms alone. Then walk into each one together. Consider yourselves co-architects and begin making plans for improving each room in the house.

The Dos and Don'ts List

1. Please study the dos and don'ts list presented earlier in this chapter in the section titled "Dos and Don'ts for Reconnecting." Now draw a circle around the "do" behaviors you know you'll have the most trouble carrying out and the "don't" behaviors you'll have the most difficulty stopping.

2. Think of each of the "do" behaviors as skills waiting to be developed. How do you do that? With practice, practice, and more practice. So, every day seek out opportunities to use these skills. For example, if it's all too easy for you to blame your problems only on your partner, then regularly ask yourself what you've done that contributed to whatever problem you're facing. And don't just ask, either. Make sure you answer your own question honestly and fully. As with any other skill, you'll find that this one gets easier and easier the more often you use it.

8

Emotional Affairs: The Internet and Beyond

My name is Bernie. I've been married for three years to Barbara. I always thought we got along pretty well, but she has complained that I don't share my feelings enough with her. Anyhow, last year Barb found a guy named Marty on one of those websites where you meet people, MySpace or Facebook, one of those sites. Now she literally spends every evening upstairs on her computer. I'm sure she's talking with Marty, but whenever I walk into the room she clicks off the page she was on and won't tell me where she's been. She says it's personal and none of my business. So now, instead of hearing her complain about my silences, I'm complaining about hers. I feel as if I've lost my wife to a complete stranger. I just don't see how we can stay married if this goes on much longer.

Electronic communication makes emotional affairs easy, tempting, and powerful. This chapter is about the emotional affairs people have completely or partly over the Internet using BlackBerry and iPod devices, e-mail, or cell phones with text messaging. Electronic emotional affairs may also include using instant messenger; chat rooms;

bulletin boards; real-time audio and video; filmed scenes; games; and social networking websites, such as MySpace, Facebook, YouTube, Bebo, and Classmates.com.

THE INTERNET IS CHANGING HOW WE MEET

The Internet is a superior source of information that stimulates us in many ways. You can explore outside your neighborhood or city and meet different types of folks than those who live in your area. Wherever you live, you can find others who share your interests. This is a significant expansion of possibility for meeting others. Here are some ways people use the Internet to meet new people.

Matching Sites

There are several kinds of social networking sites on the Internet, including computer matching sites where anyone can find a friend, an emotional affair candidate, or even a soul mate. Often, the stated intent of the sites is to match individuals who are somewhat likely to get along together as a couple. However, after the introduction, the experience becomes what you choose for it to be.

Some matchmaking websites are wonderful. They allow you to post a picture and accept or refuse communications from particular parties, and give people looking for company, including already committed partners, opportunities to meet online—instead of in a bar. You can first meet someone online and then meet at the library. For example, one couple, both of whom were divorced from previous marriages, met on such a site and, for their first date, went shopping for their children's gifts at Christmas. Another couple went to the county fair together, introducing each other to friends they happened to meet there. However, none of these individuals were currently in committed partnerships.

Social Networking

Many new models of networking are developing in electronic media.

Much of the networking formerly accomplished at a local café has gone to the Internet. The same is true of education and career training. You can find classes you can take at your leisure and ones that have "meetings" of enrolled students and discussions on the Internet. A site on fishing for walleye might link you to other fishing sites, other kinds of fishing, fish mounting, or travel sites with places to fish. Furthermore, new types of social networking will continue to develop for many purposes, including community involvement, education and career training, parenting, and traveling.

E-Mail Lists

Electronic mailing lists, such as LISTSERV, can put you in regular contact with others all over the world who share your specific interests. On an e-mail list, you sign up and then often tune in or get e-mail from that group. You can communicate with all the others through the e-mail list and see their correspondences, or you may be able to e-mail individuals outside of the list. You can find e-mail lists for things like earthquake study, nature hiking, weaving, "greening" your home, rebuilding old cars, watching volcanoes, identifying butterflies, and planting Japanese gardens. After you've been on the e-mail list for a while, you'll get to know the members. Often, there's a rule that members must stay on topic, but not everyone does, and they may invite individuals to e-mail them outside the list.

Chat Rooms

Chat rooms are widely available on the Net and provide an environment where people can carry on real-time discussions about the things that are important to them. For example, George went to a chat room run by a medical site to talk with others who understood

Parkinson's disease. Carrie used a chat room for finding other women who wanted to talk about menopause. Warren went to a chat room mostly populated by aspiring writers who shared their work. Chat rooms are formed around many activities, including social events, everyday life, pain management, and learning about dieting or nutrition.

People-Search Sites

Some websites have the specific purpose of posting information about people in order to make their activities known. Individuals and the government publish lists that make many kinds of data available, including court records, national park land taken over by big corporations, and genealogical records. For instance, Karen believes the data she finds on government and local sites will help keep her kids safe. She can check criminal records and obtain information about sexual offenders. She cherishes her children and wants to know who's around them. Civil rights protectors post data warning about threatening organizations and local rallies.

People-search sites like Classmates.com and Reunion.com focus on finding former school classmates. They're designed to help people find each other by focusing on names, ages, and degrees or their schools and graduation years. If you join, you can usually find out what many of your old acquaintances are doing. Most of these sites charge a small amount each month to entice you and your friends to join and socialize with each other by e-mail.

Self-Expression Spaces

Self-expression models are websites such as MySpace, Facebook, Bebo, and YouTube. Some of these networking sites are growing so quickly that they may soon be as large and inclusive as portals like Google and Yahoo! You can load your own website, pictures of yourself, a list of your interests, or maybe just the videos you've personally made. These are especially powerful peer group sites, many of which invite comments and contacts from new people. Once contacted by another person, you can choose whether or not to allow him or her to access your page and e-mail. These sites are used for showing you and your friends in your activities, sharing songwriting or enthusiasm for causes, and promoting yourself personally.

Similar sites that allow you to share pictures with family, friends, and other photographers are Flickr, Snapfish, and Shutterfly.

DANGERS OF THE INTERNET

The Internet is not a bad thing in itself; it's great—but how you use it can make big problems for your committed partnership and your family. Let's discuss some of the most significant dangers.

Distortion of Image

The Internet increases the possibilities for manipulating what others see and hiding what you feel because there are few real facts and physical gestures or cues to balance an impression. On the Internet one can present oneself as one wants to be seen. The writer is in control and can easily distort the information shared. Any person can build up his or her positive qualities and erase the flaws. The bottom line here is that, just as you can decide how you want to be seen and what image to present to obtain your desired reactions from others, so can the person you're meeting.

There's something we do every day that makes up for this lack of real information about the other person: human beings are very good at filling in the blanks. That means that, while we want to look good, we also want to meet our own needs. When we don't have enough real information, we look for what we want to see. We project our own wants and needs onto the screen that is the other person. For example, Jamie might write, "I want to be independent," and Robert can "hear" according to what he's looking for, perhaps either "I'm independent and don't lean on people" or "I wish I were independent, but I haven't got a clue to navigating life on my own." What you want, and how much you want to see or hear it, can completely change your interpretation of the words coming from a person you cannot actually see. Thus, there's a danger that we'll see what we most want to see, whether or not it's actually there.

Lack of Clear Rules

Electronic methods of connecting with others seem to alter all the rules of communication we're used to. On the Internet a person can see others' discussions without anyone else knowing they're present (such a person is sometimes known as a "lurker"). In some online settings, you can come and go without saying hello or good-bye. People write things more like LOL (laughing out loud), GGOH (gotta get outta here), or ^5 (high five). Teenagers often speak in little gobs of letters that make no sense to adults. And, as with any developing language, there's no definitive dictionary for these terms; they're still changing. What are others saying to you?

What's the danger in this sort of change? Usually communications are conducted with others and in groups with clear rituals. Tact is often valued. We've learned to measure our words in spoonfuls of meaning. Suddenly the rules and meanings keep changing. Computer slang can almost be a secret language. A discussion sometimes takes no more than ten "words." We have to work with new ways of communicating for some time before they make good sense to us and we know what we're doing. It's important to know how you'll use the benefits new technologies offer you. It's also your job to set reasonable boundaries for yourself, taking as much time as you need to get to know online contacts.

Chat rooms usually have an etiquette you're asked to stick with, or you risk getting kicked out. Raging at (called "flaming") or bullying another person in the room is often not allowed. But sometimes these rules break down or are ignored. For example, in Sue's favorite chat room, people became very petty and competed with each other for attention. Then the participants began forming alliances and were mean and cutting to Sue, who ended up feeling badly hurt.

Many people no longer see the importance of following the polite protocol of older and slower methods of communication. Electronic communication really is different, and it's hard to convince people of the value of following the old rules. Words and expressions are constantly evolving. Don't use lingo you don't understand, and if you don't understand someone's communication, be sure to ask what given symbols or letters mean.

WHAT RULES DO YOU NEED?

Here are some questions to think about:

What are the rules about relating to other individuals on the Internet?

What are the rules about relating emotionally to someone you don't know?

How is it possible to form a relationship with someone you've never met?

What are the rules about when and how to communicate when it's possible to break the old rules anytime without your partner's knowledge?

Illusion of Privacy

When two people are "speaking" electronically, it seems as if they're alone together. In some computer systems they can see each other and communicate directly, but each has control over his or her own camera. With electronic communication, two people can have seats on opposite sides of the ball field but seem to be sitting together. They can talk and talk, and avoid those around them. The most important thing is that the contact feels as if it's real and as if the two are talking alone together. Others can intercept the signals from the airwaves, but so what? It *feels* private. This is why electronic communication lends itself to the divulgence of private matters and feelings of connection.

Meeting in a chat room may lead to an invitation to go off together into a more-private chat room for dialogue. You may not know in advance whether the other person just wants to talk, sell you herbal preparations, or give you amateur therapy. A "private" room means getting personal. You don't know whom you're relating to or what he or she is really like.

Here's a dramatic example of what can happen when someone goes into a private chat room. In this situation, a woman suspected her husband of searching online for an emotional or sexual affair. So she went online, found her husband's profile, and wrote him herself, posting someone else's picture and a phony profile. He told her that he believed she understood him better than anyone he had ever met. After a few discussions she made a date with him to meet at a local restaurant. Her husband was astounded and ashamed when he realized the woman with the blue hat and green notebook was his wife! He rethought the idea that an online friend could understand him better than his wife.

Ease of Connection

We can connect with someone quickly, almost anytime and anywhere, if a cell phone or computer access is available. E-mail can help maintain a relationship. If that's too slow, we have text messaging. These advancements make business easier and other people a great deal more accessible. It also means that any kind of communication can occur at any time of day. This can be a problem for male and female coworkers who already have electronic contact during the workday, when that contact is further expanded to intrude into the home. An opposite-gender coworker then becomes an emotional resource.

Few Distractions

An online relationship is often free of all the common distractions of an everyday relationship, such as paying bills, cleaning house, and getting the car serviced. When you're free of distractions, it's far easier to focus exclusively on feelings. After all, the laptop user is in control of his or her laptop, and thus the relationship. The user can sign off anytime and determine whatever he or she wants to do, rather than have to become angry or annoyed at someone with different ideas about how to use the money, what color car to buy, or who should load the dishwasher.

Emotional Trance Development

Emotions are basic, strong signals used in human communication. Online communication allows people to focus on their own feelings and ignore everything else. The human responses to emotional connection can become strong pretty quickly. If you feel a certain way whenever you talk to your friend—relaxed, excited, less stressed— your body has become involved in creating an emotional relationship. As in all human relationships, hormones, neurotransmitters, neuropeptides, and other body and brain chemicals can change. Without being aware of the process, in an emotional affair, you create a kind of fantasy or trance you can enter to feel better anytime. It may not matter that you never see and physically touch your friend. There's a person you've learned about and projected your own thoughts and ideas onto. When this behavior is reinforced by the knowledge that time with that person is available anytime through your computer, you've created a kind of fantasy world. Here you believe that you and your emotions are valued and respected as you wish them to be and that someone is curious about you in just the right way.

Increased Intensity and Decreased Intimacy

There's a difference between intensity and intimacy. Intensity comes from a sharp, deep but narrow focus on a subject. It's about getting a specific need met, or experiencing a much-desired gain or loss. A person may crave intensity, which feels more like a drive toward a specific goal than intimacy does. Intimacy can be powerful but is not that way all the time. With intimacy there's a familiarity and understanding of another that includes feelings of belonging and closeness. Intimacy includes warmth and closeness based on mutual commitment as well as intensity.

Electronic communication can produce highly intense reactions and can very quickly alter hormones, neurotransmitters, and mood. High intensity can be maintained for a while, but if everything in your life were as intense as the trance of being involved in an online emotional affair, you'd soon become totally exhausted.

The bottom line is that often what feels like increased intimacy is actually increased intensity. Meantime, the partner engaged in an online emotional affair loses the real intimacy and probably some of the real intensity of committed partnership and family.

Inability to Quit

If you're in an electronic emotional affair, you probably think you can easily extricate yourself from this relationship, and at first maybe you can. As intensity increases, though, you'll likely get more obsessive—thinking about your friend more often, needing more frequent contact, and wanting to know everything about the other person. You want contact where you know you'll get a particular kind of attention, understanding, admiration, or appreciation. You may plan in advance when you can get back to the computer, and your mood may change for the better when you get closer to that opportunity. If anything keeps you from getting online, you'll likely become irritable, impatient, complaint prone, or dismissive. Ultimately you may care more about your computer contact than sorting out the everyday problems you face in your real partnership or family.

WHY THE INTERNET BREEDS EMOTIONAL AFFAIRS

Emotional affairs develop more easily on the Internet because of its element of fantasy. You can travel somewhere else without really going there. Internet rules differ at least partly from those of the ordinary world, and there's the ability to reach out with curiosity and without responsibility. You're there for the novel, not the usual.

The Illusion of Instant Intensity

As previously noted, intensity is magnified with use of instant messenger and real-time "talking" in a chat room, which is a primary danger of the Internet for those tempted to get lost in an emotional affair. Since you're writing instead of talking face to face, making personal disclosures seems less frightening or embarrassing. When you feel in control, as you are of your computer, you don't feel so vulnerable either. Still the process of mutual disclosure is intense and powerful. You may feel that your relationship with your online friend is better than any other relationship you've ever been in.

Part of the problem is that you may make disclosures you ordinarily wouldn't make at all. The intensity builds a wall of privacy and secrecy around you, a place where you can say anything. It sure feels as if you know this person inside and out.

Unintended Sexual Temptation

It's easier to slip into an unintended sexual affair when you've created an online emotional affair. Perhaps you've written to someone off and on for a long time; who'll be the first to suggest that you meet? What will you do when you have to fly to San Diego for a business meeting, which just happens to be where your friend lives? Can you resist meeting? If you meet, can you resist those sneaky erotic thoughts you've had lately? Can you clearly remember and keep the promises and commitments you've already made to your partner?

Or you may feel you have a completely new best friend and discover that the best friend you know on the Net, who goes by the name of Manhattan Marie, really lives in Manhattan, Kansas—which is only thirty miles away. This can produce both a temptation and a fear. What you've thought about, looked for, and projected onto your friend could be wrong. You may have given out a fair amount of information about yourself. You wanted a special friend. What does your friend want? Whom does he or she know? Is it possible that you and this friend could get closer in other ways? It feels so great talking to this person online; should you get to know him or her in person? What about meeting for drinks at Club 76? Your thinking can become confused and unclear.

A Quick Fix for Unmet Wants and Needs

Previously we discussed how people often enter into emotional affairs because of unmet wants and needs. When you feel frustrated, it's easy to make an "I want this and can't get it from my partner" list. From there, it's even easier to imagine that your new electronic confidant can perfectly meet your desires. When you look at the Internet as a substitute for communicating with your partner, it looks good. It looks as if everything you want could be there, free and easy.

Let's review some items from our list of unmet wants and needs with an eye to Internet communication.

I WANT MORE EMOTIONAL CONNECTION

Electronic communication offers so many different ways to establish a connection with someone. So many people are right there to "talk" to that establishing a connection with someone isn't very difficult. Linda went online to find emotional support. When Mike "met" her, he felt that they had some problems in common. She wasn't really happy, she said. Mike knew he hated his job and his boss, but he felt that he had to keep supporting his family. He didn't want to talk with his wife, Mary, about these things. However, he wanted to know that someone would be there to talk to whenever he was down. Linda and Mike began to feel more connected with each other: Mike, because he allowed himself to freely express himself, and Linda, because helping someone else made her own problems seem smaller by comparison.

I WANT MORE UNDERSTANDING

The word "understanding" illustrates what partners often want and need because when you turn it around, it changes to "standing under," which is a supportive stance. In a real-world partnership, there are lots of things to be done, and we may run short of the time it takes to understand each other as well as we could. On the Internet, what you project onto others—what you want them to be—is what you see. If it's understanding that you seek, the more the other person agrees with you, the more you may feel understood. You're looking only at similarities. You can write reams electronically, and anyone willing to read it may understand some things about your feelings or thoughts. True understanding is rare and is more about spending time with a live person who is interested in figuring out how the puzzle that is you is put together than about achieving momentary electronic connection.

I WANT MORE PRAISE AND LESS CRITICISM

At home, your partner has different habits than you do, and chances are that you're both critical in some ways that you could change. On the Internet, if you want more praise and less criticism, you're free to present yourself as you wish you were, to shine the silver a little so that others can't see your faults. Let's face the fact that a lot of what happens when communicating electronically is just talk. People who need to feel liked will find those who want praise and praise them. Whether the praise is genuine or not is up for grabs.

If your definition of more praise and less criticism is that you want to criticize your partner for not praising you and for having high expectations, you can do that, and participants in a chat room will listen and agree. But nothing will change at home.

If you want more praise and less criticism, work on praising and appreciating your partner. Notice and comment on everything he or she does that you like. Instead of finding a friend who agrees that your husband is lazy or your wife is bossy, and becoming more negative, you may find yourself thinking positively and being reawakened to your partner. You may also get more of the positive attention that you want at home.

I WANT MORE FREEDOM

If what you want is more freedom, you certainly can find it on the Internet. Freedom is at your fingertips, and if you crossed the usual boundaries a little, who'd know? On the Internet you can be who and where you want to be. Through cameras, you can travel to someone else's house and be free of responsibilities. That sounds pretty good.

However, freedom creates its own problems. Too much freedom is like too much of anything. It becomes everyday and boring. It can fill up your life until you're empty. People become thrill seekers because the adrenaline rush is all that keeps them from being bored. If you want to gain a sense of achievement, which is a more substantial feeling, be creative with your partner so you both can find a way to have more freedom and sometimes spend your free time together.

I WANT MORE ACTION

There's always action on the Internet. For instance, you can see many places you've never seen before. Through a video camera, you can fly yourself down a mountainside in a "bat suit." However, that's not the only kind of action people seek. You might also look for emotional action, such as a site where you can be totally dramatic or where someone will pour out his or her emotions to you. You may want to turn a chat room into a reality show. Meanwhile, at home you're not expressing your real feelings to anyone.

I WANT MORE EMOTIONAL INTENSITY

Emotional intensity is readily available on the Internet because relationships can form so fast through a process that's part fantasy. Your body and mind's chemical messengers may be entranced or enrapt by someone or an online situation you encounter.

It's as if you've found another world to live in, part of the time. You're less mindful of everything around you that's real.

I WANT MORE RESPECT

Perhaps you believe you don't get enough respect from your partner. If you want more respect, it may seem possible to get that through online friends. You can give respect too. In fact, it may be easier to give and receive respect when your confidant is someone you don't live with, because you don't see this person's lapses and he or she doesn't see yours. If you want real respect, you can learn more about how to get and give it with your partner.

By the way, the word "respect" comes from Latin and means "to look again" or "to look twice." We often need to "look again" at our partner instead of going away.

The bottom line is that even though there's much available to you on the Internet, you can figure out how to get every one of your needs and wants met without having an emotional affair. It's also a mark of mature adulthood to recognize that you may not be able to have everything you want right now. Certainly you won't get what you want or need without being clear with yourself about what it is. Intimacy comes most easily when you openheartedly give your partner what you yourself would like to have.

THE COSTS OF HAVING AN ONLINE EMOTIONAL AFFAIR

Negative consequences from having an online emotional affair are not unusual. Information you give out over the Internet isn't private, although it may seem so. Much of that information can be recovered, including e-mails, text messages, and uploaded photographs. The proof is found frequently in the news, where individuals are confronted with online actions from months and years ago, and their careers and home lives fall apart.

Some information can be used to harm you or your partner. In addition to simply releasing the information, a person may use it to attempt to disturb your home life, or blackmail or extort money from you. You also can be threatened or stalked, and your identity can be stolen.

Here are some potential negative consequences:

- Ignoring your committed partnership

- Being found out and embarrassed

- Losing the trust of very significant people

- Being angry and hurt that your committed partner doesn't trust you when it's you who has broken his or her trust

- Having to decide between losing your emotional-affair friend and losing your committed partner

- Learning that you haven't been there for your partner and your family, and that you've missed some important things

- Learning that you cannot always trust your judgment and impulsiveness, and feeling guilty or ashamed for breaking your promises

- Losing your reputation and the respect of others

There may be some additional costs. For example, an online emotional affair can give your confidant lots of ammunition to post on his or her Web page. This person could also post a community page that warns others about you, and advertises your deepest feelings and poorest judgments. Anything you've confided to your emotional affair partner can be shared with others—in your own words—if that person feels hurt or angry enough. Also, your emotional affair partner could contact your committed partner or your workplace. Intensity and fantasy in the electronic world can take us to dangerous places. What you think is confidential may not be.

Then there's identity theft. If this emotional affair has lasted a while, this person will know your name, probably your address and birth date, and perhaps even your social security number. This person may know where your credit card is and where you bank online.

Theft of your identity or finances can hurt you and your committed partner for a long time.

GETTING OUT OF AN ONLINE EMOTIONAL AFFAIR

The first thing you need to do to end an online emotional affair is exactly the same as if you were ending a face-to-face emotional affair. You need to make a firm commitment to end the contact immediately. There may be a part of you that wants to bargain and negotiate instead of act courageously, but your job is to say good-bye.

Saying Good-bye

Once you have made your decision, the next thing you must do is decide how to say good-bye. This emotional affair must come to an end, so the question is how to say good-bye and mean it.

It may not be easy to say good-bye and then avoid contacting the other person in any way, but that's what you need to do. Merely limiting your contact with your online friend to only once a week or one website won't work. You need to give this relationship up in order to get back to your family. Block this person's name off your list. Get rid of everything concerning this friend, and if you send a good-bye message, tell him or her to block your messages as well. If you haven't met this friend in person, you needn't meet him or her to say good-bye (despite that your bargaining brain may suggest that you do).

Note How You've Cheated Yourself

Think about the cheating aspect of this relationship. Even if unintentional, all the energy, time, thought, anticipation, and concern you've put into this particular relationship did not go into your committed partnership or family. Think about what this means, and if you're willing, ask your partner to help you make a list of when and how you were "gone," and what you missed.

Notice that you may have cheated yourself as well as your partner. If you can be very rational and clear with yourself, you'll even see how this experience has prohibited you from maturing in your ability to solve your problems. You'll be able to see how you've distracted yourself from significant issues.

You May Need to Grieve

Yes, you'll feel that something is missing. You may feel sad and miss the friend you "see" in your mind. You'll also miss the emotions that made contacting this friend and getting messages from him or her so attractive. You'll miss the anticipation when you sit down at your computer. You may want to run into the local Internet café. You may tell yourself that returning that person's text messages can't hurt anything, because you've trained your body chemistry to respond to all these stimuli as well as the person. It's time to think of the person as gone and allow the feelings of sadness and sense of loss to go through you. You'll survive this loss of your illusion.

Avoid Blaming Your Partner

With grief and loss, of course, comes anger. Guilt, shame, and misjudgment lead to anger too. So there'll be anger to deal with. But don't start by looking at your partner, at his or her bad deeds, controlling nature, or shortcomings.

Get Honest with Your Partner

Begin by looking at yourself. One very significant part of developing emotional maturity is taking responsibility for your own actions, thoughts, and feelings. No one can "make" you feel anything. The feelings you have are most often those that you choose. Nobody can make you rationalize or justify to make things right. You choose those mental behaviors too.

Get honest with your partner if you've not done so yet. Tell him or her about the emotional affair. Expect your partner to feel hurt and possibly angry, but don't run away from the truth.

Use Common Sense

Keep your computer in a public space, so anyone can see what you're doing when you use it. Don't use the computer unless your committed partner is at home. Remember that the computer has helped you train your brain to associate certain behaviors with producing certain chemicals. Avoid websites that remind you of your emotional affair and that arouse you. Find a friend to talk to who understands why you want to reconnect with your family, and use that friend as a regular contact if you're tempted to relapse.

Keeping your promises to yourself will strengthen you. And keeping your promises to your committed partner provides the underpinnings for greater intensity and intimacy in your relationship.

Concluding Comments

Long-term relationships take a fair amount of thought and effort every day just to maintain and a lot more than that to thrive. It's all too easy for things to go wrong. Best friends can gradually become disinterested roommates or even hateful enemies. That's fertile ground for one partner to begin an emotional affair, hoping that a new confidant will perfectly understand and care.

As you now know, emotional affairs are *intense, primarily emotional, nonsexual relationships that diminish at least one person's emotional connection with his or her committed partner.* The only good thing about them is that they signal that something is missing within a long-term relationship. Unfortunately, they're so destructive that their value as a messenger is far outweighed by the damage they cause to the committed couple. Emotional affairs affect the long-term relationship like acid, eating away at the couple's foundation of trust, love, and friendship. The emotional affair must end; only when the affair is over can the original partnership be repaired.

Once the emotional affair is over, the healing can begin. Of course, repairing your relationship will take a lot of time, energy, and love. Both of you will need to make and keep a lasting commitment to each other. Hopefully, the final result of all this pain will be that your relationship will emerge stronger than ever before.

References

Enright, R., S. Freedman, and J. Rique. 1998. The psychology of interpersonal forgiveness. In *Exploring Forgiveness*, ed. R. Enright and J. North. Madison, WI: The University of Wisconsin Press.

Gottman, J., and N. Silver. 1999. *The Seven Principles for Making Marriage Work: A Practical Guide from the Country's Foremost Relationship Expert.* New York: Three Rivers Press.

Potter-Efron, R. 2001. *Stop the Anger Now: A Workbook for the Prevention, Containment, and Resolution of Anger.* Oakland: New Harbinger Publications, Inc.

Potter-Efron, R., and P. Potter-Efron. 1989. *Letting Go of Shame: Understanding How Shame Affects Your Life.* Center City, MN: Hazelden Publishing.

———. 2006. *Letting Go of Anger.* 2nd ed. Oakland: New Harbinger Publications, Inc.

Random House Unabridged Dictionary. 2nd ed. 1993. New York: Random House, Inc.

Sapolsky, R. 2004. *Why Zebras Don't Get Ulcers.* 3rd ed. New York: Henry Holt and Company, LLC.

Ronald T. Potter-Efron, MSW, Ph.D., is a psychotherapist in private practice in Eau Claire, WI, who specializes in anger management, mental health counseling, and the treatment of addictions. He is author of *Angry All the Time* and *Stop the Anger Now* and coauthor of *Letting Go of Anger*, *Letting Go of Shame*, and *Reclaim Your Relationship*.

Patricia S. Potter-Efron, MS, is an experienced clinical psychotherapist living in Eau Claire, WI. She writes, teaches, and facilitates relationship workshops for the general public. She is coauthor of *Letting Go of Anger*, *Letting Go of Shame*, and *Reclaim Your Relationship*.

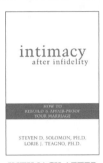
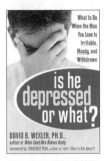